DISTRIBUTE OR DESTROY

A Survey of the World's Glut of Goods with a Description of Various Proposals and Practical Experiments for its Distribution

_____

by

BRYNJOLF BJÖRSET
(SHAMCHER BRYN BEORSE)

Translated from the Norwegian
by I.R. and E.S. de Mare

℘

THE SHAMCHER ARCHIVES

ALPHA GLYPH PUBLICATIONS

ISBN: 978-0-9783485-6-4

Library and Archives Canada Cataloguing in Publication

Björset, Brynjolf, 1896-1980
[Efter oss kommer overfloden. English]
    Distribute or destroy : a survey of the world's glut of goods with a description of various proposals and practical experiments for its distribution / by Brynjolf Björset (Shamcher Bryn Beorse) ; translated from the Norwegian by I.R. and E.S. de Mare.

Translation of: Efter oss kommer overfloden.
Includes bibliographical references.
ISBN 978-0-9783485-6-4 (paperback)

    1. Wealth. 2. Social credit. 3. Money. 4. Technocracy. I. Maré, I. R. de, translator II. Maré, E. S. de, translator III. Title. IV. Title: Efter oss kommer overfloden. English.

HB179.N62B5613 2015   330.1   C2015-903257-1

Cover Design: Diane Feught
www.distribute-or-destroy.shamcher.com

Alpha Glyph Publications Ltd.
Vancouver BC Canada
www.alphaglyph.com

DISTRIBUTE OR DESTROY

CONTENTS

Introduction

Combining the work of various "heretical" economists into one accessible volume, this book by Brynjolf Björset (later known as Bryn Beorse) leads up to a tested Scandinavian economic experiment. Nordic Clearing was established as a bridge to a new applied economy. Behind it was a radical overview dedicated to rethinking the nature of money, particularly in the climate after WWI.

In the early 1930s Björset was asked to outline the basic work of the best known new economists of the day, offering an assessment of the situation of poverty in the midst of plenty. He produced *Efter Oss Kommer Overfloden* (After Us the Glut), his world economic survey published by Aschehoug in Oslo, Norway in 1934. It was immediately translated into English, and released in Britain and the US as *Distribute or Destroy*.

This book brought the young civil engineer, Brynjolf Björset, on to the world stage as a firebrand economic thinker who applied radical theories for the greater good.

His engagement with Nordic Clearing was reprised after WWII when he was selected to participate in the group that rebuilt the economy of Norway. Even today, Norway is an example of the kind of cautious innovative economic policy that serves the community and nation over excessive private profits.

Pushed by the dire global depression, the need for a new approach to distribution of goods and services sparked a variety of innovative thoughts on the economy. Redefining wealth, re-examining the gold standard, placing the new theories into historical contexts, this book gives a great deal of information for further discussion and exploration. It is a start in building a bridge from the old world-view to the new.

Each chapter is dedicated to one economic approach that had received reasonable traction in the thinking of the times. Some had been applied, others remained theoretical, so far untested in the world.

Now almost a hundred years since some of these theories were first drafted we can look with fresh eyes at the ideas that were emerging in those tumultuous times after WWI.

Rapidly increasing production power, expanding industrial output and the revolution in electric power met both left- and right-wing political ideologies in an arena of war debt and post-war shock.

The Great Depression caused economists the world over to re-examine the economic cycles of the century past. New fermenting ideas were everywhere, but were often dismissed by the status quo as merely the wacky fringe activities of marginal cranks and quacks. Each of the systems in this book has been so vilified, yet each has a merit that brings to the fore a new approach for the future.

Björset foregrounds many of the new economists of the day, offering digests of their main tenets, with an invitation for interested parties to examine their work further. He personally met with many of these distinguished economic thinkers, and worked closely with them, not only in creating Nordic Clearing but after WWII in rebuilding the economy of Norway. Applying these concepts, the Nordic Clearing Company's regulations are listed in the appendix, for those who may wish to also create new non-gold based exchanges.

In today's age of bitcoins and other cryptocurrencies, awareness of the 99%, various small applied barter systems, and much more, we can look back to some earlier efforts. It is useful to compare our current thinking to the radical work of experimental economists who didn't have the advantage of our advanced computer systems, but whose goal was reorganization for the common good.

The re-thinking of money as a means of exchange, of wealth as use and distribution of goods, of the health of a community based not simply on stores of gold but on useful enterprise is a noble ideal to strive toward.

The original English edition included this introductory quote: "The upper limit to human numbers is not set by any facts of nature, but by human ignorance and inadaptability." (Professor Haldane in *Possible Worlds*)

It is easy to dismiss new economic theories as the nutty ideas of those who are disenfranchised or uninformed, on the margins of the mainstream. Far from the case, new concepts in the new field of economics were being tried and experimented with, either in thought or in test applications, by noted accomplished theorists, and Björset reported on these forward thinkers in this book.

Dr. Robert Eisler's book *Stable Money* is one of the main foundations of this new economic thinking, questioning the gold standard and its relation to currency. In Austria, Eisler was a well-known Jewish historian of art and culture. He was a forward thinker, and a follower of Carl Jung. This influential man was a guest professor at the Sorbonne while he was Assistant Director of the League of Nations Universities Interrelation Office in Paris, and he lectured at Oxford before the war. He later survived internment in both Dachau and Buchenwald.

The book's translator, Eric de Mare, who became a prominent architecture photographer, was a utopian thinker. A frequent visitor to Sweden, he perhaps connected with Björset at that time of intellectual ferment. Just graduated in 1933, de Mare supported New Architecture, and he looked to economic reorganization as a means to foster better architecture to provide better lives in community. He joined the Social Credit Party in 1933 and with his brother, Ian, prepared the English translation of *Distribute or Destroy*. Before WWII he was General Treasurer of the Social Credit Party in England, and over the years he wrote many inspired futuristic utopian articles about willing cooperation and a new civilization based on full employment. Many of de Mare's ideas are consistent with Beorse's vision, however, due to his strong bias, the tone of the English version of the book perhaps veers more closely to Social Credit. The original Norwegian book offered balanced assessment of various approaches, with Social Credit being only one.

The ideas of Social Credit have been discredited partly due to its mysterious morphing into a strange amalgamation of right-wing politics and evangelical Christianity–leaving behind its basis as a radical new economic system. In addition, there is a troubling shadow of anti-Semitism that still persists, based on some of the founder's statements. However, these views do not necessarily impact the idea of the system itself.

The first Social Credit articles were published in Orage's *New Age* magazine, one of the first early modern magazines of the 20th century. More interested in metaphysics than politics, Orage was a pupil of Ouspensky who went on to establish Gurdjieff centres in the USA.

Social Credit was applied in the 1930s (with some modifications) in the province of Alberta through a newly-elected Social Credit Party, led by the popular radio evangelist, William Aberhart. Its system of "currency" was short-lived, soon shut down by Canada's federal government. It should be noted that well before WWII, Aberhart expelled anti-Semites from his legislature.

In correspondence with Samuel L. Lewis in 1966, Beorse openly offers his evaluation of the founder of Social Credit, Major Douglas:

"...Mr. Taylor recently of Alberta who confirmed my impression that Aberhart and Manning, Alberta Social

Crediters, good, honest and astute men who had carried to great success, against tremendous odds, the weak but basically true ideas of social credit. Douglas, its "inventor" and champion was not very clear or wise, and his "equations" were never accepted in Alberta, luckily, nor was he ever willing to go to Alberta and see the only practical application of his theories, though he was invited while I was in London with him."

In another letter he bluntly wrote:

"Social Credit– not a good name now. John F. Kennedy was rising from ignorance to a good grasp of the main principles, until he uttered "The myth of the Federal Budget." So true, but I asked Seymour Harris, his tutor and senior advisor to the Treasury if it wasn't too blunt. "No no, just right! It had to be said." US economists now are social crediters in the right sense as those Canadians (simple) in Alberta were years ago, but you do not now have to go to Canada to learn about what is now more developed here at home. Douglas, the creator of Social Credit was much of a Babbitt, too, fond of simple mathematical formulae which did not at all fit the complex economic structure (more advanced math may be used discernedly) and refused to go to Canada to see what was really then better than him, afraid he would be embarrassed. I still have a better overall view of economics of any country but less knowledge of details, than most. But if I am appointed anywhere I can collect, digest and use the details toward a solution. It is a complicated instrument, not to be played with."

Beorse met and worked with many varied distinguished economic thinkers, and was more concerned with uplifting humanity than with the distinctions and differences that divide our communities.

Luther Whiteman and Samuel L. Lewis had quoted *Distribute or Destroy* in their book, *Glory roads: the psychological state of California* published by Thomas Y. Crowell Company in1936. Written during the Great Depression, it was prefaced as "an attempt to record only some of the better known crusades of the depression years, and to picture only some of the more important of recent messiahs." In the book they reported on the new economic groups based on the ideas sweeping through the consciousness of Californians. From *Distribute or Destroy* they included the example of the ruined coal mining village, Schwanenkirchen in Bavaria, and the adoption of Wäras system that brought it back into activity.

They may have read this book as part of the background to their endeavour. It is more likely that they added the example as an afterthought, after meeting the Norwegian Björset in California when *Distribute or Destroy* had been released in English in the US. Beorse and Samuel L. Lewis shared another connection: both had been pupils of the great mystic, Inayat Khan. They had studied with him in the mid-1920s, attending the Sufi Summer School in Sursesnes, just outside of Paris. Retaining their close relationship in the decades to follow, they continued discussing and implementing socioeconomic theories and ideals for the betterment of humanity.

It was Whiteman who first told Beorse about the Dunes in Oceano, and the naturally curious Beorse was drawn to discover more. The Dunites had not been given a very positive assessment in their book, yet Whiteman and Lewis had both spent time in that open community. Frequently visited by California intelligensia, it was fostered in part by Gavin Arthur (grandson of Chester Arthur, former President of the United States) and the Irish Folklorist Ella Young. Beorse's book, *Fairy Tales are True*, dedicates a long section to this Bohemian Shangri-la, which was home to eccentric characters ranging from hobos to yogis, writers and artists. In Arthur's magazine, *The Dune Forum*, each issue featured an article on some aspect or approach to new economics, along with the other ideas of the times that were looking toward a New Age. At Moy Mell, Gavin's cabin in the Dunes, differing viewpoints on economic directives were hotly argued. *The Dune Forum* reflects how paramount economic theories were in the Dunites' passionate discussions.

Such varied views were similarly brought together in *Distribute or Destroy*. The book introduced an everyday reader to the principles behind some of the more prominent new economic approaches being discussed in the early 1930s. The chapter "Precedent" includes a clear overview of the approach and some of the contents. From purely theoretical Technocracy to the partially implemented Social Credit system, all seen in the context of Stable Money and new approaches to the "idea" of money, the book's range showed the reader of the time how many people in Europe and the UK were thinking beyond the status quo. They were not always in agreement, but all realized the need to create something new.

Visible in the writing are the attitudes of the time, and reading this book we realize that it was in current memory of many living in the 1930s that the "horsepower" of a vehicle related to the power of a number of actual horses. The statistics quoted here reveal the rapid accelleration of production and the need for society to catch up with an effective mechanism of distribution.

At the time this book was written, the First World War is the only war mentioned, and war debt refers to its aftermath. There was no inkling of the Second War to come. Perhaps if some of these theories had been implemented, that tragedy could have been avoided.

Seen from today's vantage point, the decades between the World Wars of the 20th century were a time of upheaval and re-evaluation on every front. We are now in a similar crisis of poverty in the midst of plenty, with added looming environmental threats on the horizon. Perhaps revisiting some of the earlier radical economists can spark further innovative thinking and implementation toward active and lasting support for our global community.

In the book, Björset quotes Eisler's 1934 statement: "A great many of our economists have not yet noticed that this world of unavoidable scarcity is by now as dead and gone as the stone age."

Carol Sill, Vancouver BC, 2015

Preface to the Norwegian Edition

Superficially at least, the future of the world certainly does not appear hopeful. In spite in a few signs of recovery, that the prospect is everywhere uncertain will be admitted by the majority of those acquainted with present-day world conditions. There is, however, no denying the extraordinary possibilities latent in these times of ours.

Many schemes have recently been advanced for the utilization of our enormous potential powers of production, and for the solution of that tragic absurdity of "poverty in the midst of plenty," from which the world is suffering. The best-known of these are dealt with in this book.

Circumstances today are in general of the same kind everywhere, and it is therefore not surprising that the solutions advanced should have many characteristics in common. A study of the schemes advanced in various countries is, therefore, not irrelevant to the problem at home, for they deal with merely different sides of the same ubiquitously vital questions.

Too aggressive an enthusiasm can unfortunately be as dangerous to our evolution as over-cautiousness, And it has been my aim in this book to place an unbiased account and comparison of the more "heretical" economic proposals before the general public, without whose support no reform can possibly take place.

Dr. Ragnar Frisch, Dr. Kr. Schonheyder, professors in economics at Oslo and Bergen respectively, and Mr. Rolf E. Stenersen have among other things being kind enough to examine my manuscript and have given me hints invaluable to the final shape of the work. I am especially grateful to Mr.

Stenersen for placing at my disposal his time, his knowledge and his wide business experience. Dr. Thomas Sinding of Oslo University and Mr. Hans J. Utne, the barrister and political economist, have constantly assisted me with advice and information. Mr. Trygve J.B. Hoff, and the economist and Director of the Building Trades Association of Norway, and Mr. Holger Koefoed, Director of the Bankers' Statistical Office, though not having seen the manuscript, have both, by their extremely valuable criticism during discussion, being responsible for much that I have written.

Brynjolf Björset, Oslo, April 1934

PREFACE TO THE ENGLISH EDITION

The aim of this work is threefold. Firstly to give the reader an impression of the abundance, and especially potential abundance, of goods in the world today.

Secondly, to review the different plans put forward for the better use of existing powers of production. Only a few of the many proposals that have been advanced could be dealt with in this popular work, and it is not claimed that those chosen are the most excellent, but each is well-known and typical of its kind. To the Norwegian edition dated April 1934 much has been added, and the whole work has been revised and re-edited to bring the English edition up-to-date.

The third specific aim of the book is the drawing of comparisons and a conclusion. The different schemes are compared, and a close study will show important traits common to all of them. I believe it is possible to bridge the gulf between the standpoint of orthodox city finance and that of the so-called "heretical" pioneers, and that on that bridge we could cross to a saner and happier life. There is need of a greater mutual understanding, and it is hoped that this work will contribute to that end.

I have derived much help from the works of English and English-speaking financial leaders, pioneer reformers, scientists, industrialists and authors, to all of whom I wish to express my sincere gratitude.

Brynjolf Björset, Oslo, November 1935

Has humanity today reached the threshold of an era of undreamed of freedom and plenty, and if this is true, what is the "Open Sesame" which will admit the peoples of the earth to the enjoyment of this new prosperity?

In this book a Norwegian civil engineer reviews and compares the answers of the more advanced scientific and practical men to these questions.

CHAPTER I

OUR OPPORTUNITY

Du ring which period of history would you prefer to have lived had you had the choice—under the Roman Empire, during the Reformation, at the time of the Napoleonic wars, the present day, or a hundred years hence?

"It would, no doubt, has been very interesting to have lived during any of these periods, and even more so, perhaps, to live a hundred years hence. But I for my part am content with the present age, for there has never occurred, and never will there occur a more wonderful opportunity than is ours today of devoting all our energy to the creation of a new and better world."

This little conversation between a continental banker and himself was recounted by Sir Josiah Stamp in concluding a lecture given by him in Oslo in March, 1934.

Now, what does a man with such exceptional insight into the conditions and possibilities of the world at large mean when he speaks of a new and better world? Is he expressing conviction or merely optimism?

We are certainly beginning to hope that we have at last turned the corner, and that a part at least of the 30 million unemployed of the world will find work, but according to accepted principles we must yet continue to live in fear of "cyclical depressions" with millions again workless. Can we hope only for the crest of one of these periodic waves? Is that our "wonderful opportunity"? An increasing number of people deny this and assert that we now really have to chance of escaping forever from the so-called trade cycle, and of gradually evolving towards far fuller productivity and a far higher standard of living. Every day science has news for us of that super abundance which is ours for the asking. Technically speaking, it should be a simple matter to distribute this abundance, but human ignorance and inadaptability bar the way.

This state of affairs is rapidly changing. The reality of plenty is becoming generally recognized, and hence the psychological resistance is weakening. The time is therefore near when we shall be able to take advantage of our circumstances and increase production to its full technical capacity without violent change, and without inflicting hardship on any particular class, merely by the proper adjustment of distribution to production. Such an adjustment need not restrict individual freedom and initiative, but could, on the contrary, set free that individual creativeness which is now in fetters.

This point of view is not the outcome of hysteria induced by the present crisis; its roots are in the past, and it now has so many prominent advocates that a worldwide reform in this direction *may any day become a matter of practical politics.*

Here are a few of the many statements which have recently been made on the scene that *it is now in our power to control and forward economic development in a far higher degree than we do at present.*

Vincent C. Vickers (Director of the Bank of England from 1910 to 1919, chairman of various monetary commissions, etc.) in a foreword to a book by Dr. Robert Eisler supporting a plan for a vast credit expansion related to the industrial expansion just now possible, writes: "The existing monetary standard is unworthy of our modern civilization and a growing menace to the world–and yet there are many amongst us dreading the effort and the cost of reconstruction which is so urgent!

"When we remember the opinions and warnings of such men as the late Lord Melchett, Mr. Reginald McKenna, Lord d'Abernon, Sir Robert Horne and many more, and when we remark how chambers of commerce, agricultural and industrial organizations and other bodies, political and non-political, economic and ecclesiastical, are all reaching out in the same direction, then surely it is time for the government to seek advice elsewhere, and to encourage open discussion, rather than to attempt to shelve the question. We must realize that upon our future Standard of Value will depend our future Standard of Living. Without the establishment of a constant and equitable relationship between value and price, confidence between finance and productive industry cannot be permanently restored. But the time is short. For upon this great problem of money with which Dr. Eisler deals in so masterly a manner depends the prosperity of agriculture, and all those other productive industries upon which the credit of the country rests. Our aim should be to go forward to a new economy, not back to the old regime!"

The world famous Austrian economist, Dr. Robert Eisler, writes in his book *Stable Money,* from which the above foreword is taken: "It is unnecessary and intolerable in modern civilization that there should be widespread poverty at the bottom of the social scale. By monetary methods we can steadily raise the standard of life of the masses without upsetting the social stratification arising from historical and biological selection, and without abolishing the difference in economic potential needed to stimulate economic efforts, without the establishment of an omnipotent dictatorship, or such a moral change in human nature as is never likely to occur."

In the introduction to this work, Dr. Eisler gives a list of seventy two prominent persons who, he considers, more or less share his views.

Professor Irving Fisher, one of the best known political economists in America said at the 19th annual Congress of the American Association for Labor Legislation: "I am firmly convinced that we could almost completely solve the problem of unemployment by stabilizing the purchasing power of money. Nineteen out of twentyworkless can be said to have lost their employment on account of fluctuations in the value of money."

Professor O.M.W. Sprague, Roosevelt's former adviser, writes in an article dated 16 December,1933: "Full employment for the whole nation therefore implies that conditions must be created which would enable industry to absorb not only unemployed industrial workers, but also a great proportion of those who are today engaged in agriculture. This would seem to be impossible, but in reality industry can do it under certain conditions, for there exists for manufactured articles as opposed to agricultural produce a potential demand which is almost unlimited. This applies to the great majority of manufactured goods."

The German Swiss manufacturer and reformer, Silvio Gesell, has said: "Instead of hitting someone else's head, it would be far better to make use of your own, *by studying the nature of money!*"

He considers that unemployment, poverty and the resultant wars and revolutions are to be ascribed to faults in the means of distribution, faults which he thinks can easily be remedied. We will return later to his viewpoint.

The Scots engineer, wartime prices expert and sociologist, Clifford Hugh Douglas, writes in his book *Social Credit* (1932): "The gap between demand and supply has nothing to do with the ability of the production and industrial system to meet the calls which are made upon it; it has to do with the organization which stands in between demand and supply, that is to say the financial or ticket system. In other words, the persons who want and cannot do without the goods which the productive and industrial system can, and is anxious to, supply, have not in their possession the tickets, the possession of which is essential before these goods, under present conditions, can be handed over."

His supporter, the English barrister C.M. Hattersley, has dealt further with this point in a statistical review, according to which it would be possible to treble production in England, if this ticket system were in existence and functioning properly.

Professor Bertil Ohlin of Stockholm in an interview in December 1933 said: "Deliberate control of our economic life denotes a new phase in our development and we cannot now turn back."

Professor Ragnar Fritch of Oslo writes in his book *Sparing og Circulasjonsregulering* (1933): "It is my belief that it will not be long before the practice of controlling distribution will be recognized as a duty as imperative as that of ensuring justice."

The Norwegian agriculturist, Thor Bjerke, wrote in an article in 1933: "The first problem is to balance purchasing power and goods and the second to maintain their equilibrium. When this has been achieved agricultural laborers in common with other classes will be economically free."

Similar utterances could be quoted ad infinitum. They express a point of view that is becoming more and more general among all classes and professions the world over, viz. that the paradox of poverty amidst plenty can be attributed only to faulty organization, which it is in our power to remedy.

There are, however, an insufficient number of people persuaded of this today to justify the hope of any immediate change. We stand at the crossroads and many think that a step in the wrong direction may lead to the extinction of our civilization. The man in the street is therefore vitally affected and in the end he will have to settle the matter. Those who sit and wait for the experts to agree will wait in vain, for no single class or profession can be considered exclusively expert in this sphere. The choice of direction is in its main features simple enough for all to appreciate, even though the details may offer difficulties. But as we have seen there are experts enough to maintain that these difficulties can be overcome.

Dogmas and slogans are an ever-present danger, and they are to be found both among the untutored and the erudite. How often do we hear expressions like "free competition," "natural development," "no state interference with the delicate mechanism of finance"? A little thought will show that the monetary system is fundamentally a matter of state "interference", which relieves us of a cumbrous system of barter. In fact all who depend for their livelihood on "the delicate mechanism of finance" and on "private enterprise" indirectly owe their existence to the state and its benevolent intrusion. Of what kind this intrusion should, or should not be is however, a debatable question.

In the following pages we shall deal with proposals which claim that certain kinds of state interference can be of general benefit, as opposed to those many various contradictory interferences which at present hinder production and distribution.

The aims of the proposals vary, but a close examination will reveal so many common features that one has every right to hope for a fruitful cooperation. Moreover, they'll have the same foundation—the distribution of existing wealth and the exploitation of our present huge productive powers.

Before we examine these plans let us first consider what there is to be distributed, by taking a birdseye view of the conditions and possibilities in the world, obtained from the personal impressions of a traveler, and from various statistics and writings.

Chapter 2

The Age of Plenty

That we live in an age of plenty is an assertion that all too many would have good cause to challenge, for their lot is a hard struggle to acquire the bare needs of existence. Others, who realize the extent of our resources and who understand the statistical position, admit the existence of plenty in the case of certain commodities but deny it, probably quite rightly, in the case of others. The word "plenty" is here used in the wider sense of potential wealth, or the wealth of tomorrow, when many new and wonderful inventions which seek recognition will no longer be denied, and when the workless will refuse to continue any longer in idleness. Considering the productive power available in mechanical and human energy, abundance should be ours, and in many countries the extent of this potential abundance has even being roughly calculated.

But before turning to a tedious list of figures, I shall give a few actual instances of what I have seen on my travels.

The plains of Borneo are so fertile that the ground has only to be scratched, a few grains of rice scattered, and in a very short while the effort is rewarded a hundredfold. Part of these lowlands placed under cultivation would suffice to maintain the 30 million inhabitants of the neighboring island of Java, but for some reason it is not profitable to make use of nature's bounty in this way, although every year numbers of Javanese die in starvation.

A train of motorcars sets out daily across the Syrian desert between Damascus and Baghdad. Along the whole route lie half-buried in the sand the remains of derelict vehicles, four-seaters for the most part, which, often loaded with 14 or 15 passengers, has been literally driven to pieces. Yet motor car manufacturers are on their knees for orders and the workless alternately beg and threaten at the factory gates. The government of the country has not the means to build proper roads and bridges across the desert, yet all over Germany bridge-building firms lie dotted as frequently as railway junctions, all working at half capacity. If an order should be heard of a score of firms will swoop down, cut prices to the minimum, and make offers involving extra shifts for slaves who receive no overtime wages. On the other hand Syrian dates and oranges from these same deserts would be very welcome to weary draftsmen in engineering offices. But no exchange is effected. To be sure, enthusiasts all over the world loudly claim to know the solution of the problem, but they are never heard and their books remain unread, because everybody is satisfied that there is a depression and that, therefore, nothing can possibly be done.

In the Ruhr valley can be seen miniature mountain ranges of unsalable coal, while not far distant at the Essen foundries, bands of workers are ceaselessly engaged in turning and probing heavy slag heaps to glean a few scraps of unburnt fuel.

It is this paradox which is remarkable, the existence of a palpable surplus side-by-side with the real need—the ploughing-in of cotton when children are suffering agonies of cold, the overproduction of building materials when housing is inadequate. For instance, in 1930 Poland had a stock of 500 million bricks. A quarter of the brickyards had closed down and the remainder were working at 30 to 50% of capacity; yet housing conditions in Poland are notoriously inadequate.

"Overproduction," if taken to mean excess over needs, is a completely misleading term. As Professor Soothill of Oxford wrote in an article in the *Times*: "The talk of overproduction would be amusing if it were not so pitifully circumscribed. There is no overproduction of anything of value to the people of the world."

We hear that there is an overproduction of wheat, yet in

northwest China millions of people have within recent years died of hunger. Much has been written lately of the colossal overproduction of boots and shoes in Germany. Actually during 1931-1932, 0.96 pairs per head were supplied to the population as against 1.04 pairs during 1930-1931 and 1.14 in 1924-1925, while before the war a normal annual output in England for the home market was approximately two pairs per head. Yet in 1931, 24% and in the following year 32% of the workers in the German industry were unemployed, while during the whole period output was about half the productive capacity.

It is therefore obvious that a surplus is unconsumed, not because there is no need for it, but because there is a deficiency of purchasing power–and purchasing power is the link between production and consumption. Were this deficiency caused by unwillingness to produce and consume, certain economists would be justified in asserting that the lack of purchasing power reflects a reality; the desire to produce and consume is there, but a faulty economic system hinders its full expression.

The Austrian economist and historian, Dr. Eisler, writes: "The science of economics itself it developed during the long ages of scarcity. Therefore 'economy' became synonymous with the difficult part of economizing material and energy. The theory of capital and interest was treated as if the productive capital was built-up only by saving and not by spending. If it had not been for the pressure of want and scarcity in all human activities, economics as a science would not exist today.

A great many of our economists have not yet noticed that this world of unavoidable scarcity is by now as dead and gone as the stone age. [author's italics]. And the reason for the lack of perception is simply that their master, Adam Smith, laid the foundations of modern economic doctrine in 1759, 25 years before James Watt perfected the steam engine—"

Now, what actually could be produced and consumed were the mechanism of distribution in working order? C. Marshall Hattersley in his book, *This Age of Plenty*, claims the production in the British Isles has been assessed at one quarter of what it might be. It can safely be assumed that at least three quarters of this maximum output could be absorbed. In other words it would be possible to treble the yield of agriculture and industry in England, if purchasing power were adequate.

H. L. Gantt has computed that production in the USA today is 1/20 of capacity. Again reckoning with a 75% potential demand it would be possible to increase effective production in that country fifteen-fold. Other American writers have assessed this possible increase at 900%. These figures are, of course, to some extent speculative but their scale is significant.

For the whole world collectively, production has been variously estimated at between 1/5 and 1/10 of capacity. *In other words, the general standard of living could be increased from 5 to 10 times were it not for a defective system of distribution.*

There is an inclination to think of a higher standard of living purely in terms of material advantages, but since, for example, no one can eat more than three meals a day, the demand for primary commodities must naturally be limited. There is, however, no limit to the demand for culture and luxury, for art, travel, and social amenities of all kinds.

In a world of such great productive power, there exist 13 million unemployed, even though in England, for example, an increase of nearly 20 to 30% in production would be sufficient to give work to everyone in the country.

The realization is growing that there is an inherent fault in the system of distribution, and that very little of permanent value can be effected merely by meeting periodic slumps with emergency legislation or by leaving the individual to muddle along in the hopes that things right themselves. Even if the present crisis were mitigated somewhat, is it certain that all the unemployed would be absorbed?

In answer to this question, let us take two typical examples of what the immediate future holds in store, quoting, as an introduction, the following extract from C.M. Hattersley's work, *This Age of Plenty*: "The possibilities inherent in the application of science to agriculture are by no means exhausted in enabling the soil to yield four or five times the crop produced in the 18th Century, or in continually extending the food-producing areas. We are today on the verge of discoveries whereby vast quantities of food stuffs not at present suitable for human consumption maybe transformed into substances easily digestible by mankind."

In confirmation of this sweeping promise, our first illustration is taken from Professor J. B. S. Haldane's book *Possible Worlds:*

"Plants make sugar from carbon dioxide, water and sunlight. A few like the potato store most of this in starch, or some other form that we can digest. But the majority of them convert it into cellulose, the main constituent of wood.

"The cow and horse can no more digest cellulose than ourselves. No animal nearer to us than a snail can make the enzymes requisite for even a partial digestion of it. But an ungulate is a cooperative society. It consists of the mammal which forms the façade, and some millions of millions of bacteria engaged in breaking down cellulose. The products which they form from it are largely digestible by the horse or cow, but would be unpalatable if not harmful to man. However one of the intermediate stages in their production from cellulose is an easily digestible sugar! When– not if– we can separate the cellulose splitting enzymes from those which break up the sugar further, we shall be in a position to convert woodpulp or hay quantitatively into human food.

"This is one of the facts which render dubious all prophecies as to overpopulation. The upper limit to human numbers is not set by any facts of nature, but by human ignorance and inadaptability."

Food direct from tree stumps! Boom times for lumbermen! But what of the farming population? Will they will come unemployed among their numbers, or will this discovery, like so many others, be suppressed in the "interests of agriculture"? But why should human drudgery be fostered when it ceases to be necessary?

At the Chicago World's Fair the general public was introduced to something which had long been familiar to the building profession– the standard house, mass-produced in factories from insulated steel or copper. The procedure is simple. An order is telephoned to the manufacturer for new house, type B5, No.II. In a few hours it arrives on a couple of lorries accompanied by two fitters, who assemble the parts in a twinkling. Payment is on the installment plan. Now if this is the trend of building development, results can only mean the increase of unemployment among cabinetmakers, masons, carpenters and bricklayers. But, it will be objected, the machines, which disgorge these houses, must be made and operated. Certainly, but only partly by human labor. Delicate apparatus, sensitive to light and sound, will keep a keen watch on irregularities and will automatically control the machinery. These same "photoelectric cells" apprehend thieves in the night, keep a tally of the men as they come to work in the morning, do the work of policemen, watchmen and lodge keepers. Even in the offices, where men pore over columns of figures, the ranks are being thinned. Not only ordinary comptometers but complicated bookkeeping machines, which work accurately, quickly, without complaint and without the least tendency to abscond with the cash, are taking over human jobs.

"Everlasting steel" is no longer a fiction. A razor or a motor car lasting a lifetime could in fact be produced, but these inventions are withheld on account of existing plant.

With the above instances, I have tried to illustrate that plenty which nature, hand-in-hand with science, has to offer us. The 1,800 million inhabitants of the world have at their disposal a stream of energy (such as solar and atomic energy, which may perhaps prove to be identical) far exceeding that needed to supply all their imaginable wants.

It is the sole function of economics to set about converting this energy into useful things and distributing them. A recognition of this simple fact would work wonders in the world today.

CHAPTER 3

PRECEDENT

Are all our present difficulties due only to the new conditions imposed by vastly increased productivity and a surplus of commodities, or is this only one side of the question? Are there features of the present crisis which have a general significance, with analogies which can be found in the past?

The mention of history will put many readers on their guard, for as the old saw says, history can be interpreted not in one but in 50 ways, all of them contradictory. Others will be reminded of the words the politicians and economists repeat with such complacency: "There have been crises before and they have passed over. History proves it. This crisis will also pass, if we have patience."

It is surely this type of man the veteran economist, Stephen Leacock, addresses when he says: "Our studies consist only in the long-drawn proof of the futility of the search after knowledge effected by exposing the errors of the past. Philosophy is the science which proves that we can know nothing of the soul. Medicine is the science which tells us that we know nothing of the body. Political economy is that which teaches us that we know nothing of the laws of wealth."

In spite of these warnings let us nonetheless look at the faults–and the merits–of the past. I do not intend to trace here the chronological development of economic history, but I will touch only on certain periods which have had a special bearing on our subject.

Good and bad times are phenomena as old as history itself, and when minted coins were first introduced into ancient

Greece in 750 BC, booms and slumps begin to alternate with a certain regularity. There have, however, being periods which were essentially free from financial crises, as, for example, the so-called European Renaissance, roughly between the years 1150 and 1400 AD.

It is claimed that in spite of all depressions and difficulties we in our day have every reason to congratulate ourselves on the consistent rise in our standard of life. This rise is certainly true of the last 100 or 150 years, that is to say, the so-called industrial era, although the least fortunate today are worse off than at the beginning of the era. But if we consider earlier periods as, for instance, that between 1150 and 1400, we find a standard of living for which even the more prosperous among laborers and artisans today would envy, a period, be it noted, when productive power per individual was a fraction of what it is now.

A study of this fabulous age, and other times of depression which followed it, may possibly throw some light on the subject of trade cycles and their causes.

Professor Damaschke writes in *Geschichte der nationalökonomie* (Jena, 1905): "The period between the years 1150 and 1400 is an unusual one, a period of such general prosperity as we today can hardly imagine," and France in *Der Weg der Kultur* (Berlin, 1905) writes: "I think I have proved that in the 60 German free cities, in the hundred municipal republics of Renaissance Italy and in the 250 towns of ancient Greece, humanity can be said to have reached the state of the greatest possible well-being. In each case the race attained a wonderful heyday, such as we can hardly credit."

We learned that agricultural workers in Renaissance Germany, that is to say the ordinary day laborers, earned from 6 to 8 Groschen a week, which corresponds to 70s and 90s at the present cost of living. Calculated on the same scale journey men earned the equivalent of about £5 a week and there keep, or £8 pounds a week without it. A skilled workman could earn up to £10 pounds a week with keep or £15 without. In many places Monday was a holiday, the so-called "Blauer Montag."

This was a social club day, when military exercises were practiced. Apart from this about 90 fast days were observed during the year, so that there was an average working week of only four days. Furthermore on these four days working hours were regulated. When in 1465 the Duke of Saxony attempted to increase shifts in his mines from 6 to 8 hours, he met with strenuous popular resistance.

A great number of towns grew up during this period and with them many of the grandest churches and castles of middle Europe, including for example the Marienburg–"Germany's proudest castle" as it has been called.

The spacious and happy existence of the peasant class during this time in Central Europe is described in Gustav Freitag's *Bildern aus der deutschen Vergangenheit.*

Middle European currency of that age has been found in Nordic countries, which shows that the north took a certain part in the lively international trade of the time. We have not sufficient data, however, to judge how conditions here compared with those of central Europe, but accounts of the great prosperity enjoyed during the reign of Hakon Hakonsen indicate a similarity. In 1350 the Black Death put an end to whatever glories existed, and on the continent also these flourishing times came to an end during the 15th century.

"Whence came this reaction which led to a cleavage of the church, the 30 years war, the French revolution, the world war and jazz?" asks Fritz Schwartz in his *Die Brakteaten, das zweckmässige Geld des Mittelalters.* He continues: "Throughout the whole of the Middle Ages the people waged a bitter fight for the so-called 'Denarius Perpetuus', the everlasting coin, which does not sustain any change during the course of the year. Money was wanted which could be accumulated, and not only serve as a medium of exchange. This demand was eventually met. A start was made in Augsburg and Freiburg by postponing the withdrawal of coin for several years. In the end this withdrawal stopped altogether, and the value of money became constant. Then one district after the other followed suit.

"Thus the growth of monetary capital became possible, a thing which before was practically out of the question, on account of the constant withdrawals which acted as a tax on ready money."

"With this rise of money capital," Fritz Schwartz continues, "the means of exchange disappeared into the savers' stockings, mattresses and chests, and as a result became scarce in the labor market.

"Historians of today never tire of condemning these withdrawals of money. At the same time, as we have already pointed out, they are at a loss to account for the economic blossoming and the refined culture of the two centuries in question. They are equally puzzled by the opposition of Austrian towns to the issue of 'heavy coins'. They do not understand it *because they cannot differentiate between a means of exchange and a means of accumulating wealth* and believe that both must, and can, be combined as money. It is, however, impossible simultaneously to save money and circulate it as a means of exchange."

With the reintroduction of money which could be accumulated, the rate of interest rose, and difficulties increased for all who laboured. The schism in the church can certainly be partly attributed to this fact. The people lost confidence in spiritual leaders who failed to champion their battle against high rates of interest. Their circumstances grew consistently worse; for instance the miners mentioned above had to give way to the Duke of Saxony and accept an eight hour shift instead of a six hour one. Luther and Zwingli both strongly opposed high rates of interest. A contemporary political writer, Sebastian Frank, wrote: "The sort of traffic now pursued among Christian merchants, companies, usurers, and moneychangers is patent even to the baby in its cradle. There is continual speculation, buying ahead, and a flooding of the country with the useless rubbish, to the detriment of the people. Many wonder why there is not more money in the land. Others, who think more clearly about these matters, are surprised that we manage to support ourselves at all, such as conditions are."

Fritz Schwartz continues: "Today, however, we are on the point of again introducing the good old Gothic currency, a pure means of exchange, as opposed to the Greco-Roman means of accumulation."

Fritz Schwartz is a prominent figure of the Central European economic movement, "Free Economy," and what is meant by this promise of "introducing the good old Gothic currency" will be explained in the following chapter. The pioneer of this movement was Silvio Gesell, a businessman who became active as a reformer during the 1890s. The Free Economists have based their opinions to a large extent on his studies of the Renaissance, and as the Free Economists have in their turn influenced many other economic movements, the period is of special interest to us in this review.

Other theories have been advanced to account for Renaissance prosperity. The so-called Georgists who date from the middle of the 19th century, ascribe it to the conditions of land rent, and consider that all subsequent crises, including our present depression, are the result of the private ownership of land. They do not wish to abolish the right of privately cultivating land, but believe that benefits derived from an appreciation in ground values should accrue to the whole community.

This principle has been adopted by the Free Economists, but they maintain that by far the more fundamental consideration is the organization of distribution, which was far better adapted during the Renaissance than it is now to the production and distribution of goods, which were available and for which there was a need. Their object is to base money on credit, that is to say not on a single little-used commodity such as gold or silver, but on the aggregate of commodities, the proper distribution of which is the true function of money. That is to say, they wish to so organize the mechanism of distribution that money and credit will serve production, and be in a constant and proper proportion to real productive power.

The theories of the Free Economists have become

known in America, chiefly through the works of Professor Irving Fisher, and they have thus influenced the Technocrats, whose economic proposals are very similar to those of the Free Economists.

At almost the same time as that of the Free Economists a similar movement was started in England, which had for some time no name. Mr. Arthur Kitson is regarded as its pioneer.

These "New Economists" in England do not follow the Free Economists in their particular proposals, but their object is the same–the correlation of real wealth and productive power to the means of exchange.

One of the problems which Arthur Kitson has especially studied is that of saving, a very topical question today among political economists. It is, therefore, interesting to note that Arthur Kitson said as long ago as 1905 that: "to save money is one of the earliest lessons one has to learn. But there is nothing more certain than that this custom if it were practiced as much as it is preached would ruin a great part of the world's industry, and considerably lower the general standard of living. A big demand cannot be created unless people are willing to spend. Abstention from certain things, such as alcohol or other poisons can be preached without harm. But those who agitate for as great an abstention as possible from all those things which nourish, support, beautify and ennoble life, merely for the sake of saving, teach a lesson which is in the highest degree destructive and dangerous, both economically and socially."

Professor Frederick Soddy, who counts himself a successor to Arthur Kitson, says also that the more freely people as a whole spend money, the more there is available to spend, and the less they spend, the less there is available.

A contemporary of Professor Soddy is Major Clifford Hugh Douglas whose views are somewhat similar to those of Arthur Kitson. Douglas concentrates especially on the influence of industrialization, of the machine, on the economic life of the community.

His doctrines have given rise to an economic school with a fairly wide organization, by the name of Social Credit. This school, in common with the previously mentioned movements, wishes to base the amount of money and credit in existence on the actual productive powers available. What differentiates this movement from most of the others is the proposal to issue money not only to the producer but also, to a certain extent, direct to the consumer.

In this respect Social Credit is supported by Technocracy, which came into being as a public movement in America about 1930. Technocracy is based on the investigations begun in 1920 by a number of scientists and technologists into the economic and technical conditions and possibilities of the USA.

It was between the years 1920 and 1930, also, that the Austrian authority on economic history, Dr. Robert Eisler, in the service of the League of Nations, made definite proposals for the expansion of production in a certain group of countries with a corresponding expansion of credit. He also submitted a very detailed plan at the World Economic Conference in London in 1933. Many orthodox economic experts and politicians supported this proposal, among them being Mr. Vincent C. Vickers.

With Dr. Eisler we come to the very large group of economic performers, whose ideals can be summarized under the heading of "Stable Money," and who desire as constant to price level as possible, i.e., a constant value of money in terms of the average price of goods. Writers in this group will differ very much in their opinions as to how a stable price level may be reached, and of course other measures must be adopted before a rational system of distribution can be hoped for. The stable money movement is over 100 years old. Among its present champions it includes J.M. Keynes, Sir Josiah Stamp and Reginald McKenna in England, Gustav Cassel and Bertil Ohlin in Sweden, and Franklin D. Roosevelt and Irving Fisher in the USA.

The common contention of the proposals which have been summarized here, and which will later be more closely considered, is that before social conditions can be bettered not only must production be reformed, working hours, wages and so on, but also the whole system of money and credit.

A considerable number of schemes of this kind have been advanced. A German association which set itself the task of collecting them, discovered over 2000. The proposals here discussed are therefore a small and possibly a fortuitous selection, but they are the best-known and the most typical, and provided general aspect of a matter, which would be impossible to study in detail. The great number of schemes advanced, though intimidating some people and amusing others, should not be a cause of disparagement, for in the first place the problems involved are vitally important, and in the second thing made miss of a great many solutions. Moreover many have much in common.

Other suggestions, which seek to remedy without essential changes in the mechanism of distribution, may be roughly grouped under three headings:

1. Employment (in increased public, and, eventually, private works).

2. Shorter working hours (including earlier pensionable age and longer a compulsory education).

3. Increased wages (and prices).

Proposals prominent in politics during recent years can as a rule be assigned to one or more of these three categories.

The question of work is the first one to be considered when a crisis comes with its restricted production and unemployment. Already during the war the Labour Party in England had elaborated a scheme for the absorption of those workers who would be available at the conclusion of the war, and in 1928, when unemployment reached the million mark, the Liberal party propounded a plan for the direct occupation of 500,000 men in the construction of telephone installations, power stations, roads, etc., the idea being that the remaining 500,000 unemployed would be absorbed through the stimulus imparted by these public works to the whole economic life of the country.

Neither of these plans was adopted– for financial reasons. Although both the labor and the means of production were available and the work was both useful and necessary, the system of distribution prevented its execution.

In America, Germany, Italy and Sweden such schemes have been partly carried out, but not by any means on a scale sufficient to make use of all available labor–again on account of financial considerations. Big schemes in Norway have also had to be abandoned for the same reason. Many excellent smaller enterprises have actually been carried out, but they have been as drops in the ocean.

"Shorter working hours" are often suggested, either through a shorter working day, or week, or through the limitations of the number of working years by means of a later school-leaving age or by earlier pensioning. This latter method has be much discussed in France among various political parties.

From a purely humanitarian point of view this is sound enough, but though it may become so in the future, as a solution to the present crisis, it is neither justifiable nor practicable. In the first place there is still plenty of work to be done in the world, at all the available power, and more would be needed did the system of distribution allow necessary development. In the second place, reduced hours of work at the same rate of pay, meaning reduced weekly wages, would result in a lower standard of living than the existing one for the working classes, and would certainly not benefit industry and agriculture. Increased rates of pay with shorter hours, on the other hand, would mean higher prices without a correspondingly higher aggregate of wages. Hence a lower standard of living and a smaller output of goods would result. Under our present system of distribution reduced working hours would therefore be no palliative and it is for this reason that the remedy has not been extensively adopted except in America.

The third group, higher wages, means increased costs and usually a rise in prices proportionately greater than the rise in wages, i.e., actually a reduction of real wages. The converse method of first raising prices can sometimes effect a temporary improvement but it has on the whole brought only disappointment. A rise in prices all along the line means a fall in the value of money in relation to goods, and it is doubtful whether any permanent improvement and social conditions can be attained through constantly fluctuating prices.

Quite another matter is the proportionate adjustment of wages or of prices between different industries. This is often both justifiable and effective. In recent years, for instance, the prices of agricultural produce have sunk far lower than the average price of manufactured articles and the state of the farmers has become desperate. In such a case, the regulation of prices in favour of agricultural produce is a vital necessity, not only for the farming population, but for the whole community, whose economic balance is destroyed by such anomalies.

It is, however, equally certain that this kind of price control is alone not sufficient to bring supply and demand into a proper relationship.

Another method which has been cited as a solution of both the agricultural and the general crisis is collectivization of farming—the grouping together of specialist farms under a depot or centre which would be responsible for their joint administration, selling, local equipment, transport, etc. No doubt this is in tune with the times, but it does necessarily provide a solution of the present.

The increased profitableness resulting from this would no doubt give enterprises more value and thus increase the aggregate of credit and the rate of turnover of goods, but up to the present, at any rate, the reverse has usually been true. Financial conditions have hindered the organization of this type of unit. On the other hand, a rational system of distribution would make even the old fashioned farms profitable enough.

Thus we can conclude that, in general, the proposals during the present crisis all fail at the same place—the system of distribution, and we must fall upon those older ideas which, born in less distressed times independently of sudden crises, deal with the nature of distribution itself. Earlier in the book the prophetic words of Fritz Schwarz were quoted: "Today we are on the point of again producing the good old Gothic currency."

Let us now consider an experiment which has been made in this direction.

CHAPTER 4

THE FREE ECONOMISTS
(THE SWISS PHYSIOCRATS)

*I regret that I have been too busy to attend to your inquiry of the 19th
July before today.* These are the opening words of a letter
to me signed "H. Hebecker, Mining Engineer" and dated
"Schwanenkirchen, the 10th September, 1933." This Hebecker
was in 1930 an out-of-work mine-owner without a working
capital, living in an impoverished country town which lay in a
district devastated by the financial crisis. At that time he was
certainly never "too busy." From whom, then, did he obtain the
capital he needed? The answer is—from nobody; he created his
own capital, out of paper and on the credit of future production.
The explanation is contained in the following adaptation of
two newspaper reports published in Germany in March 1931:

THE MIRACLE OF SCHWANENKIRCHEN

"In Regensburg we were told that up in the Bavarian
woods just beyond Deggendorf there lives a man who prints
his own money. His notes, which are called 'Wäras' are said
to be used by the whole neighbourhood, which has become
practically independent of the Reichsmark.

"After learning that the man with the private printing press
is named Hebecker, and his money paradise Schwanenkirchen,
it was not long before we were standing in the presence of the
enterprising gentleman himself.

"In itself a Wära is not remarkable. Mr. Hebecker drew
one from his note-case, and was kind enough to sell it to me
for a mark. Later I made a little experiment; after lunching at a
restaurant in the neighbouring town of Hengersberg I handed
the waiter my Wära in part payment of my bill. He accepted
the note without a murmur.

"The Schwanenkirchen mine produces lignite, coal not of the best quality, but which should nevertheless have a ready sale so long as Germany needs fuel. At one time the town of Deggendorf ran the mine, which supported the inhabitants of Schwanenkirchen, Hengersberg and Schöllnach. Later a limited company with all its complicated paraphernalia took control, failed to show a profit and ceased operations in 1927.

"Hebecker bought the concern when it came under the hammer, hoping to be able to work it himself on a modest scale. But he could find no one willing to finance an undertaking in such an outlying district.

"For years the workings were derelict and the water rose fifty metres in the shaft. The young men of the district trod the stony path to the poor-house and the engineer lived alone by the side of his waterlogged mine. This went on until the autumn of 1930, when, as the rest of the world was sinking under the weight of the great depression, a miracle occurred. The pumping apparatus was set in motion, the plant repaired and work recommenced in Schwanenkirchen colliery. Trucks again rattled merrily over the funicular. The poor-house was emptied of its sixty despondent occupants; shops and inns reopened; the whole place assumed a busy, hopeful air.

"I made inquiries among the inhabitants as to the cause of this turn in their fortunes. The good Bavarians could answer me only vaguely that a mysterious gentleman, as if by the wave of a magician's wand, have suddenly brought about the revival. Mr. Hebecker himself explained matters to us as follows:

"As the works-engineer employed by the former company I obtained the mine for 8000 marks, and, though it was worth many times that amount, no bank or trust company would finance me. At last I turned to my friends the Physiocrats, who gave me 50,000 Wäras, with which I was able to start operations.

"And what are Physiocrats and Wäras?'–you will ask.

"The Physiocrats are a group of people who aim after reform of the monetary system in accordance with the principles laid down by Silvio Gesell, their founder. One of their fundamental principles is that money shall have, not a lasting but a shrinking value, that is to say it shall depreciate at a certain rate. At present the advantage of money as a means of saving consists the fact that, whereas most commodities lose their value over time, money is a fixed quantity.

"The Physiocrats wish money to function only as a means of exchange, having no other cover than confidence in the creative industry of the community which uses that, and they believe that a constantly depreciating currency by increasing the velocity of circulation creates more values than one with a constant "value", which spells speculation.

"For propaganda purposes the Physiocrats put into use within their own circle such a means of exchange, naming their unit the Wära. The monthly depreciation is 1%, which can be made good by the application stamps.

"There is a printed explanation on the notes to the effect that they have no cover and that they cannot be redeemed. They are, therefore, not currency and on this account they have been safe from the attention of the public prosecutor and the Reichsbank.

"I made it plain to the Physiocrats that my mine was an excellent opportunity for propaganda. They understood the position, gave me 50,000 Wäras and the wonder began.

"I called the old miners together. For years they had been unemployed. I told them that we could start up again, but I had no money, but something that was just as good, if only they believed in it, namely Wäras. The miners looked at the yellow notes and came to the conclusion that it was not so much a question of their confidence in them as that of those tradespeople who catered for their needs. First of all, therefore, I had to set up the canteen, stocked by suppliers in central Germany, who are members of the Physiocrats' organization. Naturally enough after some weeks the tradespeople at the district were only too ready to come to terms.

"Since then our new monetary system has worked

splendidly. With Wäras I have reopened the mine, given occupation to 40 colliers, established trade connections, if only in three country towns, and at the same time given practical proof to Physiocrats of the efficacy of their system. In this neighborhood nobody any longer believes that the Gold Standard is our only salvation

"'It is interesting to remark that the 'Rentemark' was introduced to Germany in much the same way as was the Wära in Schwanenkirchen: on confidence, not in the value of the paper notes but in the value of the goods and services they represented.

"Orthodox monetary experts will most certainly not be in favor of the Schwanenkirchen experiment. Nonetheless Mr. Hebecker's mine produces coal while the whole economic system of Europe is crippled; and though such a comparison might be thought frivolous, it need not necessarily lack significance.

"The question now arises: how can a private individual issue his own money, which has no relation to the established currency? To be sure during the inflation every town in Germany issued its own emergency currency, which was accepted in business, but those were quite abnormal times, and today the private issue of currency would be strictly illegal. The explanation is that Wäras, these extraordinary yellow notes, simply are not money. The Wära is no more than a means of exchange; it cannot be money in the technical sense since it does not fulfill the two main conditions of money: it has no cover and it is not redeemable. It is a means of exchange, issued by the Wära Exchange Trading Company with registered offices in Berlin. Schwanenkirchen adopts a system of barter by means of these yellow notes, and, strange as it may sound, experiences of revival of prosperity.

"A strange experiment, this Wära oasis in the forests of Bavaria, where a fantastic theory has in a modest way become a reality. What will happen to it? Will the Ministry of Finance step in, or the Reichsbank? For the present there is no noticeable interference; and the natives, who have suffered so much, cling with full confidence to this straw and are glad to be able to work and live again."

So much for the journalistic account. The Wära was actually launched as long ago as in 1926 as a means of exchange within the organization of Physiocrats. It represents the practical application of the theories of the Swiss businessman, manufacturer and agriculturalist, Silvio Gesell. It was in 1930 that the Wära notes first attained any economic standing in that they financed Hebecker's mine and the surrounding district. Not long afterwards they were to be found all over Germany. Large firms in Berlin, Bremen and other cities announced that they accepted Wäras as payment; even a number of savings banks accepted Wäras as interest-bearing deposits, making themselves responsible for the monthly depreciation. On certain shares in the Schwanenkirchen colliery there was a minimum guaranteed dividend of 10%.

On 31 October, 1931, the Wära, in common with all other emerging means of exchange, was forbidden by the Breuning ministry, "in view of the general distress." But the mine which had been started with Wära money was nevertheless kept going, although with difficulty, and thus one small district at least had reason to remember with gratitude this short-lived but gallant monetary experiment.

As young man Silvio Gesell migrated in 1886 to the Argentine, where he founded his own business. Five years later he published his first book on monetary matters. In the meantime he had had experience of the harmful results of alternating periods of inflation and deflation caused by governmental interference. He argued that if the volume of circulating money increases more rapidly than the volume of goods for general price level rises, and, as long as this rise is expected, money continues to be spent more quickly, and a boom period in business is the result. On the other hand, since the value of money falls, debtors benefit at the expense of creditors. If the volume of circulating money decreases in relation to goods, the price level falls, people spend reluctantly and eventually an economic crisis may result. At the same time creditors benefit at the expense of debtors. Both these movements always harm one part of the community. This can be avoided by adjusting money and its control to the needs of modern commerce.

If only the volume of money is increased to correspond to that of goods, the result is increased savings and investment in interest-bearing securities. An increased supply of capital creates lower rates of interest with the consequence that money is withheld from circulation. This forces the banks to issue more money. But this money can with impunity in its turn be saved and withdrawn from circulation. On the rumor of a scarcity of goods it can, furthermore, be suddenly released in large quantities and cause serious disorganization.

This is why Silvio Gesell suggests the use of a depreciating currency, which would be in everybody's interest to circulate. Money would then be on equal terms with commodities, which also on the whole depreciate in value with time, and it would be as advantageous to spend it as to accumulate it. The value of this money would be fixed in terms of a certain range of goods. In many ways it resembles Technocracy's "energy certificates," which I will deal with later.

In 1898 the Argentine government had embarked on so consistent a deflationary policy that Silvio Gesell was of the opinion that it would mean the ruin of industry and business. Having addressed a letter of warning in vain to the government he sold his business and returned home. In the Argentine things turned out as he had foretold.

In Switzerland he took up agriculture and settled down on a model farm, using what were then new fertilizing methods. Right up to the time of his death he lived in constant warfare with the government and the national bank, since he was ceaselessly trying to convert them to his views. These were, however, destined to meet with better appreciation in another direction after his death.

In connection with a book by Professor Irving Fisher of Yale University, entitled the *Illusion of Money*, a competition was organized for the best and most constructive critique of the existing monetary system. Over 1000 entries were received and were submitted to a jury composed of American economists, bankers and industrialists. Of the European competitors two were prize winners, Professor Ohlin (a Swede) in Copenhagen and Fritz Schwartz (President of Switzerland League of Free Economists), whose treatise consisted chiefly of a report on Silvio Gesell's theories and life's work.

Later came in the famous case of the burgomaster of Wörgl in the Austrian Tyrol, who introduced to his town "Arbeitsscheine," which were a means of exchange on the same principle as Wäras. The consequence was an amazing economic revival in Wörgl and the surrounding district. It was as a result of the success of this experiment that Professor Irving Fisher introduced the so-called "stamped dollar" to a number of American communities.

The merits of Free Economy as an economic system are sometimes judged only in light of the Wära experiment. This is wrong, however, since Wära notes were used as a supplementary means of exchange beside the Reichsmark. The official currency of the country founded on Gesell's principles would be backed by real wealth, since the notes would have a definite value in relation to a number of prime commodities. Such a currency would thus be anchored to "index numbers."

CHAPTER 5

AN ENERGY THEORY OF WEALTH

The economists of today, and before them all the sages of the past, have repeatedly attempted to impress upon us the difference that exists between real physical and cultural wealth, on the one hand, and money or credit, which are claims on this wealth, on the other. Humanity, however, has frequently failed to recognize this necessity and such states of confusion have had widespread and often catastrophic results. At the present time it is more necessary than ever before to arrive at a clear understanding of what wealth is and of what precisely is meant by money.

This age might be called the age of energy, and wealth has often been defined simply as energy. There are numerous excellent treatments of this subject by professional economists, which are too well-known to warrant discussion here. Less well-known, perhaps, are the writings of those who have both had first-hand experience of the phenomena of energy, such as scientists and engineers, and have also studied the matter from the angle of the political economist. Such a writer is Professor Frederick Soddy, originally prominent as a chemist and now as an economist, author of that stimulating work *Wealth, Virtual Wealth and Debt,* to which he has given the subtitle "An Energy Theory of Wealth and the Virtual Theory of Money." As this one book has deeply influenced very many of the "New Economists" and "heretical schools," its importance cannot be overrated.

When a scientist and Nobel Laureate in chemistry like Soddy launches into political economy many might perhaps expect to recognize in his works the sober, methodical, not to say tedious, research worker. The reader of *Wealth, Virtual*

Wealth and Debt will find that the contrary is the case. The book might in fact be compared to the work of an exceptionally volatile Impressionist painter; the whole appears to lack point or plan. A closer study of the book, however, will reveal behind its exuberance a lucid and methodical train of thought; this is the insistence of the trained scientist on a proper distinction between natural physical realities and the standards of value set by the human mind.

Professor Soddy calls money "virtual wealth," that is to say something which has only the appearance of wealth. The possession of money implies a claim on wealth, a right to goods and services, but money in itself is not wealth. This consideration might seem of little interest to the layman, for whom money and wealth in the modern community must have approximately the same significance, since there always exists the sufficiency of goods and services into which money may be converted. Looked at from a different angle, however, the distinction is plain enough, for, if we assume that money and wealth are identical, we must arrive at the conclusion that the earth's riches are made up of the total of all sources of energy, plant and commodities, plus all the money in existence, which is absurd. Obviously the wealth of the world can consist of no more than the goods, plant and sources of energy in existence. Money indicates only a right to a certain amount of this wealth, a means of transferring it from one possessor to another. On the world's balance sheet, therefore, Professor Soddy asks us to picture all sources of energy, goods and machinery, as being the sole assets. Money, as a kind of certificate, a means of distributing these assets among the shareholders, must be shown on the other side, a liability *which must balance the assets.* Hence we arrive at a definition of the function of money: it must serve as a ticket system for goods, services, energy, and its volume must accurately correspond to the wealth available. All other considerations must be subservient to this all important function.

Professor Soddy has very definite views on the subject of saving. When a man, he says, accumulates a portion of his earnings in the form of money, instead of in the form of motor cars, houses, etc., it implies on his part a voluntary provisional renunciation of goods, a relative abstinence. By means of this abstinence more machines maybe bought, industrial enterprises financed and instruments forged, which cannot be immediately consumed but which lead to an increase in capital wealth and productive power. It is one of Professor Soddy's fundamental principles that no new industry can be created except for the comparative abstinence of one or more members of the community. If a new industrial undertaking is launched without such previous sacrifice, it must be made subsequently.

Professor Soddy admits that our present money system was intended to interpret this principle of saving but he radically disagrees with those who claim that it actually does do so. Today our abstinence from consumption has assumed ludicrous proportions; it is a forced, and involuntary abstinence, because our money system has, thinks Professor Soddy, ceased truly to reflect real wealth. Wealth has, in fact, come to be measured not in goods and services, but in gold or currency, which stand in no definite proportion to those useful things into which they may be converted. The actual result of this system is such that we are forced to meet overproduction with reduced wages, more goods with less purchasing power. We are, indeed, busily sawing through the branch which supports us.

Hence the questions arise: how does money come into existence? By what standard is the volume of currency measured and why is it very frequently inadequate for production and distribution? Can central banks not create new money simply by issuing new notes? They can of course, but banknotes, however, are only a fraction of those means of exchange which today function as money. It is credit that actually forms the greater part of our means of exchange and this credit is created by the banks. Under the heading, "The Pyramiding of Credit" in his work, *Wealth, Virtual Wealth and Debt,* Professor Soddy writes as follows:

"Before the war it was considered 'safe' for the banker to

keep some £15 per £100 of cash against deposits. That is, for every £100 deposited £15 of cash sufficed for the small cash demands, most of the depositors' purchasing power being exercised by cheque. We may take this 15% for purposes of illustration only. It is doubtful if as much has been necessary for a very long time.

"Thus, dealing throughout with averages, against the original depositor of £100, £15 of legal tender must be kept in the till, leaving £85 available to be lent to a borrower. It is true this borrower might demand it in cash, but, on the average for him no less than for the original depositor, only 15% of cash or £12 15s. is necessary, leaving £72 5s. free to be lent to a second borrower ... So it goes on until each £100 of original cash becomes a total of £666 13s. 4d.

"...If the truth were known it would probably be found that this estimate is altogether too modest. At least since, if not before the war, the figures suggest rather a 7% "safe" limit than 15%. On this basis a client depositing £100 pounds of cash and current account enables the bank to loan £1330 pounds."

The Oxford economist, R.F. Harrow, in his treatise *Currency and Central Banking,* assesses this "safe" limit for English banks at from 9.5% to 10.5%. In Norway 10% is usually cited as the norm. Hugo Bilgram, in an article contributed to the *Journal of Political Economy* in 1921, assessed the cash reserves of USA banks at 8% of the total volume of money and credit in circulation. According to Dr. Robert Eisler, the Danatbank in Germany had at one time cash standing to its account of the value of only 2-3% of money lent.

Continuing his argument Professor Soddy shows that, by issuing credit means of exchange, which now forms by far the greater part of all means of distribution, the banks have usurped the former prerogative of the state to issue money. This has only gradually come about. At one time gold was generally placed in the care of goldsmiths and when clients of one goldsmith did business with each other their custom was to instruct him to transfer the sums in question to his books, by which means an actual transportation of the bullion was avoided. Later arrangements came to be made between different goldsmiths enabling their respective clients to trade with each other in the same way. These were the beginnings of the modern bank and check system. As industry expanded and with it the need for credit, paper values came far to exceed both the value of the circulated gold and that of the notes in circulation. This was a natural and necessary development since industry could never have been expanded to its present dimensions had there been no method of also expanding the volume of money. But, as we may see today, the procedure was not sufficiently scientific and this improvised issue of means of distribution has more and more shown itself to be inadequate in meeting the needs of industrial development. Only at certain periods is there an apparent agreement between money and goods, between industry and the means of distribution. These periods are interrupted by "crises," when, in spite of a surplus of goods and vast potential productivity, the mass of consumers are hardly able to afford the barest essentials.

Whether we are for or against nationalization in general, therefore, we may perhaps agree with Soddy that a state organization should see that the volume of means of distribution constantly stands in proper proportion to the available supply of commodities and to actual needs, in order that that which really can be produced and for which there exists a real demand, may also be distributed. This problem cannot be solved by a number of private and partially independent banks, who are forced by the vital interests of themselves and their clients to make the volume of credit subject to the demand for capital, to the question of interest and to purely financial considerations of profit, etc.

Professor Soddy's first proposed reform is therefore that the right to issue and withdraw all means of distribution shall again be vested in the state, whose function shall be to ensure that the volume of money and credit issued shall correspond to productive power. The objection will be raised that productive power cannot be accurately measured. An accurate measurement, however, is not necessary. Today, for example, anyone will tell you that real productive power is much greater, some will say many times greater than what the volume of money actually restricts it to. We could perfectly well afford variations in the volume of money and credit caused by an in adequate knowledge of potentialities. What we cannot afford is to allow the volume of our purchasing power to float meaninglessly in space, having no relation whatsoever to the supply of goods and the possibilities of production.

Under Professor Soddy's scheme the banks would issue loans as heretofore, but within the bounds set by the state authority for the total volume of credit. Essential industries, which could not afford to pay interest of the banks' rate or for some other reasons could not obtain credit in the usual way, would be directly financed from the communal credit pool, paying interest at the rate they could afford. Furthermore repayment of such loans would be made only to the extent to which costs of these industries were actually refunded through the sale of goods and not until after the goods have been paid for by the consumer. By this means a proper circulation of money would be assured.

At present the state itself borrows money in the open market and pays interest at the rates imposed in the market. In as far as such loans are devoted to state-controlled industries in competition with private enterprise this is perhaps equitable. Where it is a question of administration itself, of justice, education, the civil services, this arrangement can hardly be justified. Such activities are of the same order as essential industries and ought not, therefore, be charged with ordinary rates of interest. Here again the system of direct state financing suggested by Soddy would apply.

Hence we come to Professor Soddy's second proposed reform, viz., a gradual liquidation of public debt with the new money or credit issued by the state. Public debt and the interest on it is thus canceled. In lieu thereof the banks obtain cash which gives them a right to goods and services, or which may be devoted to fresh production. Either course would stimulate turnover and the wheels of trade would revolve freely again. ("Social Creditors" hold that the state in these circumstances should abandon all industrial and commercial activities, in which it would enjoy an unfair advantage owing to its prerogative of issuing means of exchange, and should limit itself to purely administrative functions.)

Many will argue that pure administrative costs are met, not with the proceeds of public loans, but through taxation. A valid objection, were it accurate! But who would seriously contend that ordinary revenue and duties levied on unnecessary commodities do not today go to the payment of interest on, and amortization of, public debt? And conversely, what local authority has not at some time borrowed money for building roads and schools, etc., which has not expected to yield interest at market rates?

Our troubles today cannot, in Professor Soddy's opinion, be overcome by "saving" and "rationalization of public expenses." (This in spite of the fact that Soddy is one of the most staunch upholders of the principle that all production must be financed through initial saving.) They can be overcome only by coupling money to commodities and potential productivity, that is to say, by issuing a new purchasing power when new useful goods are put on the market, neither sooner nor later, and by generally removing those conditions of our present system which make possible dangerous fluctuations in the volume of money. This cannot come about, thinks Professor Soddy, unless the state's authority regularly fixes the aggregate value of all means of distribution. The banks would thus enjoy complete liberty with the exception that they would not have the right to restrict or expand the volume of means of exchange, a task which they have neither the knowledge nor the ability to perform satisfactorily, and from which they themselves would no doubt be glad to be absolved.

According to a review published in 1933 by one of the largest firms of stockbrokers in Oslo, about 8 1/2 milliard dollars were loaned in 1929 to brokers in New York against deposited securities. In June 1932 this amount had shrunk to 380 million dollars. Over the same period the volume of credits in the whole of the USA decreased by about 15 milliard dollars. The ravages of the depression on the economic life of the USA are well known. This instance illustrates Soddy's point that without corresponding natural catastrophes or physical loss a restriction of credit brings about a low level of purchasing power, which is artificial and which forces production and distribution down to a desperate level. Naturally other factors play their part, as, for instance, the willingness to buy on the part of the public. The faster money is spent the greater is the velocity of circulation and this increase affects prosperity and prices in the same way as an influx of additional money. Conversely saving on the part of the public during a time of depression aggravates the general situation. These two tendencies, a desire to buy or a sudden need to save, can usually be found to be the direct results of either the issue or withdrawal of bank credits, as the case may be. We cannot but agree with Soddy that our monetary system more resembles a concertina than a means of distribution.

The above is necessarily only a short sketch of Professor Soddy's account of the problems—wealth, debt and the issue and withdrawal of money. There is much in his writings that I have not even touched upon, as, for example, the so-called "fictitious loans" and their effects. I have thought it fit to exclude from my review this delicate and intricate problem, as I consider that it has as yet been too little elucidated by experts to be publicly discussed with advantage, at any rate here in Norway.

In the conclusion of *Wealth, Virtual Wealth and Debt* Soddy summarizes under 22 points his views on wealth, debt, taxation, the function of gold (in international transactions), the possibility of a currency with index value, the transition from the present system to a state control of credit, etc. He also writes therein as follows:

"The stinging-nettle of economics need no longer obstruct the path of the social reformer who would give peace and economic freedom to the world. Its power to sting resides only in silly confusions which the world has outgrown, and which, in a scientific and mechanical age, even a bright child might be trusted to see through...

"With adequate knowledge of the physical realities that dominate the economic affairs of peoples, the road is clear for unlimited progress and the attainment of universal peace and prosperity."

To sum up, Professor Soddy's two main proposals are:

1. That the right to issue all means of exchange shall refer to the state,

2. The liquidation of public debt with the newly issued state money.

As these two proposals occur under other forms in the works of nearly all the "New Economists" their significance is considerable.

CHAPTER 6

TECHNOCRACY

Technocracy! The word has an ugly sound. It suggests the dictatorship of technique and technicians, and the inhuman mechanization of the whole community. The grim drawings of robots on the covers of the Technocrats' magazines certainly give this impression. Yet, the leading Technocrats assert that they mean something quite different by this word. They mean two things—firstly, a technical and scientific investigation of the social mechanism, which is today undeniably of an extremely technical nature, and secondly, on the basis of this investigation, technical and scientific reconstruction of that mechanism in accordance with the changed needs of the new industrial age, so that it shall stimulate production and distribution, and thereby considerably raise the general standard of living. This would enable us in our increased leisure to indulge those individual tastes which the old craftsmen, for instance, expressed in their work. It should not now be necessary, they think, always to buy what is cheap and tawdry, nor to hurry and scurry from morning till night to make ends meet. With machines to slave for us, we stand today, did we but know it, on the threshold of an age of culture, perhaps even greater than that of Greece. In fact, the Technocrats are idealists.

Technocracy was born in 1920, when at the suggestion of a young Virginian technologist, Howard Scott, a group of engineers, architects and scientists headed by the professor of engineering at Columbia University, Rautenstrauch, embarked on a general survey of the economic and industrial conditions of North America, its stage of development and its future possibilities.

The idea was inspired among others by the American economist Torsten Veblen, and by Professor Fredrick Soddy, and there is no doubt that the Free Economists and Professor Irving Fisher have also influenced the Technocrats. Moreover, they owe much to the previous investigations of a committee appointed for a similar purpose by Herbert Hoover. The findings of these two bodies are often confused.

A weakness of the Technocrats was, from the very beginning, the one-sided composition of the group, in that it consisted only of technologists, scientists and architects. The statistical material and the statements which they have published and even more so, their constructive proposals, betray this one-sidedness.

For 10 years the group worked in silence. It is claimed that through their investigations they were able to foresee the crisis of 1929. At last sensational news of the mysterious group began to leak out to the press and towards 1930 Scott considered that the time was right to publish certain statements, though many of his colleagues were of the opinion that he should have waited till they have progressed further in their research.

The first official announcement was made in a long speech by Howard Scott, at the banquet held in his honor in New York, and later he published a booklet, *Introduction to Technocracy,* which he called the "only authorized presentation." The many other books, articles and pamphlets published can thus not lay claim to be the original opinions of the Technocrats. In 1932 for instance, a leaflet which was alleged to be the work of the Technocrats, and which enjoyed a worldwide circulation, bore the following caption: "Thirty millions out of work next year or $20,000 income for every family, which do you choose? A question put by Technocracy, the bloodless revolution!" This, in view of the widespread misery prevailing in America at the time, was a grim jest indeed.

In his booklet, Howard Scott says nothing about $20,000 income per family, but merely states that a high standard of living could be assured in the future for the whole population by the introduction of rational methods. The figure of 20,000 can nevertheless be ascribed to the unofficial communication of one of the original Technocrats and was intended only to indicate what should be possible from a technical point of view, if no account is taken of the "human element."

Howard Scott's public announcements aroused so much dissension in the original group, that the Technocrats were from then onwards divided into two groups, the one being led by Howard Scott, and the other by Professor Rautenstrauch in collaboration with, among others, the engineer Basset Jones, Leon Henderson, and the architect, Frederick L. Ackerman. This latter group claims that its supporters number a quarter of a million, divided into 70 local divisions.

The essential difference between the two groups is that the one, under the leadership of Howard Scott, has advanced definite plans for a transition into energy certificates as a means of distribution, while the other under Professor Rautenstrauch objects to the advancement of any constructive scheme for the present, and only wishes to continue the original investigations. The statistics which the Technocrats have published are, however, based on their common investigations.

The Technocrats' figures have been criticized from many quarters. A certain Simeon Strunsky, for instance, wrote a long article on the subject in the *New York Times* magazine. It has, however, been impossible to find the figures he here ascribes to the Technocrats in any of their official information, and they come apparently from an uncontrolled source. Those of the Technocrats figures which I have had occasion to check, I have always been able to verify.

The Technocrats found that during the 6000 years preceding 1880 AD, which was an era of manual labor and manpower, the production and consumption of energy per head had consistently been fairly equal. But they maintain that there is now consumed in the USA about 75 times more energy than in those years before 1800 and that most of this increase has occurred since the year 1900.(One of the biggest machines in use today is equal to the power of 9 million men!) They claim that the reason for the benefit of this huge increase in the real wealth has not accrued to the population in the form of a correspondingly higher standard of living is to be found in the faultiness of the mechanism of distribution, which, since it was created for an age of scarcity, is now obsolete. As Howard Scott writes, a modern factory does not hesitate to scrap obsolete methods and introduce modern machinery, but in the sphere of economics we cling to a system which is more than 50 years out of date. We spare it on the grounds that it is much too delicate to touch.

To illustrate the difference between the economic standing of the USA today and that of 100 years ago, when agricultural produce, i.e. foodstuffs, was the essential of all wealth, and absorbed the main part of all the output of energy, the Technocrats show in their statistics that in 1933 agriculture represented only 7% of all energy output, 93% going to the satisfaction of other needs–light, warmth, transport, and so on. They accordingly claim that the cry "Back to the land!" must be discounted, for, if the 93% of energy output were abandoned, and only agriculture retained, an automatic wholesale extermination of the population would naturally follow. As Howard Scott writes: "The progression of a modern industrial mechanism is unidirectional and irreversible. Physically it has no choice but to proceed with the further elimination of toil through the substitution of energy for man-hours."

The Technocrats have illustrated the nature of this tendency toward reduction of human labor with many striking instances. In 1924 for example, an average of 1291 hours of human labor were needed for the manufacture of a motor car. In 1929, 92 hours of human labor where necessary for the same work. In order to produce one ton of steel in 1900, 70 hours of human labor were necessary and in 1929, only 13 hours.

"What is the use of the distributive system today which bases its purchasing power only on working hours?" asks the English Technocrat, Mr. Arkwright, and he then points to the Technocrats' constructive program –the basing of purchasing power on the quantity of goods in existence and on the power of production, not on working time, since in this age human labor is becoming of less and less important in production.

The Technocrats consider, in fact, that if we persist in the conception purchasing power should be given only in exchange for work done, which is an obsolete moral outlook inherited from the age of scarcity and manpower, we can expect only world chaos.

The results of the present system is that those goods which are produced but cannot be bought by the would-be consumer, become an unsalable glut and business becomes debt ridden. Here are two instances published by the Technocrats, which illustrate the general indebtedness of industry: In 1903 the General Electric Company supplied the Insull Company with the Curtis turbine. In 1909 it was scrapped as being out of date, though in working order. Later it found its way to a museum for old and strange contraptions. Full interest is still being paid on the money with which it was bought in 1903, and also on the loan which was raised to pay for the new turbine. The future is mortgaged in the same way. In 1931, a Railway company borrowed $310 million for expansion and new stock. The terms of the contract are such that there will still remain $199 million owing in the year 2047, when the engines and rails will have long since become scrap iron.

The conclusion which the Technocrats have reached is particularly interesting; it is that over a given period debt increases more rapidly than production, and both increase more rapidly than the population. The ratio between debt and the growth of the population increases with time by the second power; that is to say, in the course of two years for example, this increases four times as much as the growth of the population, in three years nine times as much. The debt of industry in the USA in all interest-bearing securities was estimated in the autumn of 1933 at 238 milliard dollars, while the national credit was estimated at 300 milliards. Debt was therefore as much as 80% of the national credit. According to a recent estimate (Fisher), the national wealth is now less than total debts. In other words, "wealthy America," from the point of view of bookkeeping, will own nothing at all! The Technocrats claim that this is one of the main proofs that the present economic system no longer reflects real wealth, for obviously America is richer now than ever before. (Compared with the debt of industry, War Debts are a mere bagatelle, and therefore there is really no foundation, say the Technocrats, for the claim that War Debts are the cause of the crisis.)

Now this "insurmountable debt" would not in itself be harmful, if it were not allowed to hinder production and consumption and keep whole peoples in poverty. There are but a few financiers who think that this debt can ever be repaid, or even that the interest on it can be paid. The only way that it could possibly be borne would be through steadily expanding markets. But when examination reveals that debt increases more rapidly than goods can be produced, it becomes obvious, say the Technocrats, why they stand for abolition of our present system.

Officially the Technocrats offer no definite solution to the problem, but state only facts. Privately, as we have seen, a number of them have advanced concrete plans for a new system of distribution. These desire the complete abandonment of the present monetary standard. They want the community instead to issue notes based on the amount of energy available, expressed in "calories" or "ergs"; they would thus correspond to a certain amount of work done, as, for example, that needed to lift the grams' weight a certain height. It is now possible to measure fairly accurately the energy expended on production by a community in one year.

The means of distribution used would be "energy certificates" which would be distributed every week or month to all members of the community, and would get the possessor the right to buy goods and services, the "prices" of which will be calculated on the amount of energy expended in each case. Thus a constant measure of value would be attained and debt and interest would vanish.

The constant objection is—how can such things be

measured as the advice of the doctor, or the art of the singer, for instance, in "energy output"? Obviously to do so directly would be impossible, but it would be possible to measure the prices of these services in energy-certificates just as accurately as they are at present measured in dollars, which have such and such a gold value. For example, the relation between a measurable piece of work and doctors' fees today could be directly transferred to the technocratic system.

Some of the Technocrats have wanted simply to distribute an equal number of certificates to all. They defend this on the moral grounds that though everyone is not of equal worth, it is impossible to determine the true "worth" of each individual, and since plenty would be the lot of all in the coming age of abundance, they consider that everyone would be satisfied by this arrangement.

But account must be taken of the many who need the stimulus of increasing material gain in order to give of their best. For the sake of these, many Technocrats would like at least part of the notes to be distributed in the form of piece wages on a tariff scale.

The validity of the certificates would be limited to a certain district and to a definite period of time, after which they would not be renewable. They could therefore not be accumulated.

"The technologist examines our so-called standard of measurement, the monetary unit–the dollar. He notes that it is variable. Why anyone should attempt on this earth to use a variable as a measuring rod is so utterly absurd that he dismisses any serious consideration of its use in the study of what should be done," says Howard Scott.

The Technocrats advance three reasons among others why the present money and price system is completely unsuited to the needs of modern industrial society:

1. Purchasing power is distributed to the public in exchange for working hours, although science is steadily reducing working hours for the same unit of production.

2. The price system forces manufacturers to reduce the

number of workers rather than to redistribute the working hours, and keep the same wage scale. Machine power is displacing manpower. The allotment of purchasing power on the basis of working hours therefore creates an increasing discrepancy between purchasing power and prices.

3. On account of the expanding outlay on machinery, necessitated by the increasing speed with which it becomes obsolete, manufacturers are forced to cut down the cost of labor. This again prevents the increase of wages and the redistribution of working hours.

The following figures illustrate the point. The height of American productivity occurred in the year 1929, but the maximum of working hours occurred in 1918. From then on, human working time steadily diminished, in spite of the rise of production up to 1929.

In the last few years the curve of working hours has dropped considerably. In the spring of 1933 there were 12 million unemployed among America's 123 million inhabitants. If the curve continues in its present direction, 20 million unemployed must be reckoned with in two years' time. Only if conditions improve, and production increases enormously, will working time show any appreciable increase, since additional labor saving interventions are inevitable.

The need of adopting a system which would make use of the enormous powers of production and allow the radical shortening of working hours all along the line is therefore obvious.

Mr. Arkwright writes: "We do not hesitate an instant to abandon an obsolete turbine, but with a death grip we hold on to a long obsolescent system of price and profit.

"As technology presses forward in industry an increasing number of functions are taken from human labor and there remain a world of goods, a world of debts, and a world of human workers with neither food nor clothing nor the money to pay for them. In this desolate pass, as though these misfortunes were not enough, we are watching now the plundering of a continent and heedless waste of its resources. Where are we to obtain the iron ore for the future? One eleventh of our steel production goes into the making of tin cans, which after use are flung onto the garbage dump. Is such a waste anything less than insanity? We are squandering our oil, and the end of the supply is already in sight; we are squandering our coal, lumber, iron, raw material and finished goods, flinging them away in the pursuit of profit that is doing the price system to death.

"The truth is that modern society has been made over into a huge and highly integrated machine; it is in effect a mechanism. If this machine is to be run in this age of high power with any degree of success, it must be run with rules that derive from the nature of the machine itself, not from a system of economics in which exact measurement is impossible.

"How is this thing to be dealt with? More cries for public works, debt holidays, and loud demands for cheap money—all palliatives. These frantic attempts to stave off the evil hour are going to avail us nothing. It is needless for us to expect anything from the Republicans or the Democrats, the Fascists or the Socialists or the Communists. They are all harnessed to price —price in different guises perhaps, but price it remains."

Howard Scott says: "Is it not obvious that the machine is an agent of freedom when each of America's 35 million workers has 3000 indefatigable slaves at his disposition, since to each worker accrues 300 mechanical horse power, equal to 3000 manpower, the machines needing only 2 eight hour days' attention per week?"

The following is a series of excerpts from Howard Scott's publication, which illustrates the Technocratic attitudes towards the present system.

"Under a price system wealth arises solely through the creation of debt. In other words, price system wealth consists of debt claims against the operation of the physical equipment and its resultants.

"To be physically wealthy is not to own a car but to wear it out. Technology has introduced a new methodology in the creation of physical wealth. It is now able to substitute energy for man-hours on the parity basis that 1,500,000 foot-pounds equals one man's time for eight hours.

"National income under the price system consists of the debt claims accruing annually from the certificates of debt already extant.

"Physical income under technological control would be the net available energy in ergs converted into use-forms and services over and above the operation and maintenance of physical equipment and structures of the area.

"Individual income under a price system consists of units that are not commensurate with the quanta by which the rate of flow of the physical equipment is measured, and upon which the social mechanism depends for its continuance. Individualism is therefore favored under a price system, since individualism can obtain a monetary equivalent proportional to the individual's ability to create debt. Individual income under such a system therefore depends on the extent to which advantage is exercised by means of the interference-control that is dominant throughout the whole system of the debt creation.

"Individual income under technological control would consist of units commensurate with the quanta by which the rate of flow of the physical equipment is measured throughout the entire continental area. The unit income of the individual would be determined by the period necessary in that area by the time it takes for a complete cycle of the operating and production procedures to be completed.

"Any unit of *value* under a price system is a certification of debt.

"Any unit of *measurement* under technological control would be a certification of available energy converted. Such units of certification would have vitality only during the balance load period for which they were issued. This message eliminates debt and philanthropy."

Howard Scott concludes his book, *Introduction to Technocracy* with the following: "All these things are entirely sufficient to ensure the continuance of a high energy standard of livelihood for at least 1000 years.

"The progression of a modern industrial social mechanism is unidirectional and irreversible. There is no choice but to proceed with the further elimination of toil through the substitution of energy for man-hours. There can be no question of returning to pre-machine or pre-technological ways of life; a progression once it started must continue. Retrogressive evolution does not exist."

The work of the Technocrats can be summed up under two headings:

1. The statistical demonstration of the industrial development of America and partly of the rest of the world, and of the disproportion between the requirements of modern industrial society and the present method of distribution; also the demonstration of the rapidly increasing difficulties which this disproportion calls into being.

2. The constructive proposals of a certain group of the Technocrats for the substitution of the present monetary system by one based on the volume of energy available.

As Howard Scott says, a dollar is worth one thing today and another tomorrow. A unit of energy is of the same worth yesterday, today and forever. The Technocrats base their whole system on the fact that all goods and services are measurable.

One of the few serious criticisms of Technocracy I have read is that of Professor W. F. Ogburn of Chicago. He writes: "I see no such collapse of the capitalistic system as they (the Technocrats) set forth. It has displayed weaknesses, particularly regarding the flow of money and credit–and it was thrown out of gear by the war. Then, also, the flow of capacity to purchase should keep pace with the capacity to produce. These are two present weak spots. But the economic organization is a fairly tough one, and there is no reason to fear collapse...

"Mechanical inventions move faster than social inventions, and the only thing is to step up social inventions to bring about adjustments."

But surely the professor is begging the point?

E. H. H. Holman of St. Paul writes: "I personally believe that the best system for establishing prices would be one based on labor hours. By that I mean the actual amount of time required to produce a commodity."

This point of view is of course akin to the Technocrats' energy system, but, when applied to this machine age, it has just that fault which the Technocrats attack. Steadily increasing speed of production and decreasing human labor for the same unit of production would necessitate incessant corrections of such a standard of value.

This and many other observations show that the main significance of the Technocrats' work and ideas does not stand or fall by the comparatively small circle of Technocrats themselves. They have elucidated certain broad principles with which all thinking people agree, such as the existence of poverty amidst great potential and even actual abundance, and the obvious cause of this—the lack of purchasing power.

Many are under the impression that the Technocrats desire a sudden revolution, and it is this idea of which has aroused so much bitter resistance to them, a resistance which is unreasonable, since they advocate a gradual substitution of obsolete methods.

It will be seen that the Technocrats are in line with all those movements which are fighting for a rational distributive system.

CHAPTER 7

SOCIAL CREDIT

By the term "Social Credit" is meant credit issued strictly to serve the needs of society. According to the program of the movement this implies two things.

Firstly, like the other distributionist theories, it implies the issue of a sufficient volume of credit to correspond to the goods and powers of production available at a given time. Secondly, it implies a definite method of allocating this credit. It must, of course, first be issued to the various productive centers. What is peculiar to Social Credit, however, is that it would distribute credit partly direct to the consumer. Shortly expressed, the argument in favor of such procedure is as follows:

How are the necessities of life produced? By agriculture and industry.

How are these necessities transferred from the producer to the consumer? By a means of exchange called money.

How does the consumer obtain this means of exchange? As wages for his work, directly when he works on a farm or in a factory, and indirectly when he or she is, for instance, a civil servant, doctor, teacher, or housewife.

Agriculture and industry have thus two functions:

1. to produce the necessities of life, and

2. to give us the means of purchasing these necessities.

Apart from this they must pay their way and show a profit, which in these times of keen competition means that costs must be kept as low as possible.

The question is—can these three requirements actually be coordinated?

To keep down costs, the fewest possible workers must be employed, at the lowest possible wage. That is to say the purchasing power issued becomes less and less capable of absorbing the products of industry and agriculture. This is the state of affairs today. More than an adequate amount of goods can be produced, they cannot be disposed of.

It therefore follows that a distinction must be made between the two functions of producing the necessities of life and distributing the sufficiency of purchasing power. The latter function demands the employment of this as possible and, indeed, drawn to its logical conclusion, the abolition of the excavator and a return to the pick and shovel, or even to bare hands! (This method is, in part, actually being resorted to in the building trade in Germany.) In short, it means the suppression of mechanized industry and a return to manual work. But is this desirable or, indeed, possible?

According to Social Credit, the means of escaping from this vicious circle is to relieve agriculture and industry of their responsibility as the sole creators of purchasing power and to issue direct to the consumer that necessary purchasing power which is not circulated in the form of wages and earnings.

Social Credit considers that the majority of people labor under a prejudice which is becoming more and more dangerous as the mechanization of industry increases—the conception that only work gives one the right to buy goods, in other words that "he that does not work, neither shall he eat." It is, however, not the amount of hours of human work, which should today be the measure of purchasing power, but actual productivity and the goods and services in existence. To distribute as much purchasing power as there are goods, or potential goods, is the only rational object of a sane economic system.

This argument is supported by an extensive documentation made by Social Credit writers on various industrial and agricultural fronts. It is, however, but one aspect of its doctrine and is the fundamental economic consequence of that sociological outlook, that philosophy of life, which in a number of writings has been advanced under the name of Social Credit. It is not a philosophy according to the ordinary humanitarian pattern, but it is a typical child of our modern industrial era. It has, however, by no means a technical or industrialized stamp, but is founded on a belief which can be expressed in the words of the American Declaration of Independence as "the inalienable right of man to life, liberty and the pursuit of happiness," which modern conditions obviously allow. It is an outlook different to that "tooth and claw" attitude which is everywhere strongly influencing political and social life. It may be said to combine the finest of humanitarian ideals with the scientific facts of modern industrial society.

The founder of this movement is the Scots engineer, Major Clifford Hugh Douglas. He was for many years manager of the Westinghouse Electrical Company's depots in various countries, but during the war he became a government price expert. While working in this capacity he noticed the widely divergent relationship between the flow of credit and money before, during and immediately after the war. He himself claims that these observations have had a considerable influence in shaping his point of view.

Shortly after the war, he published his first book *Economic Democracy,* having previously written articles and lectured on the subject. Since then he has published other works, of which the last two, *Social Credit* and *The Monopoly of Credit,* together with C.M. Hattersley's *This Age of Plenty,* give a fairly complete picture of the matter.

The movement has now a large organization in England with Major Douglas as President, and the fact that its members are of many different professions and sympathies has served to provide the movement with a general and comprehensive outlook.

There is also an existence in England, New Zealand and Australia an organization called the Green Shirt Movement for Social Credit which, though often cooperating with the various groups around the country, is of the opinion that Social Credit can become a reality only through the organized and disciplined mass pressure of the working class. It is largely composed of young men, is decentralized and uses what it terms "an unarmed military technique".

There are several periodicals which expound the doctrine of Social Credit, such as *The New Age, The New English Weekly, Prosperity, Social Credit,* and the Green Shirt paper *Attack*.

In several of the colonies and dominions, Social Credit has a stronger support than in England itself. In Sydney University, for example, books relating to the scheme are regarded as excellent economic literature. It was calculated that in New Zealand during 1934 Social Credit had the support of one in every four of the population, and in the province of Alberta in Canada the population is said to be almost unanimously in favor of the Douglas scheme.

In 1930, as a result of pressure from various non-political organizations, Douglas was consulted by the MacMillan committee. His advice is to be found in *The Monopoly of Credit*.

Recently, Douglas and his coworkers have prepared draft plans to illustrate how Social Credit would work in practice. Among these is a scheme for Scotland (included in the book, *Social Credit)* from which an excellent understanding can be obtained of the main ideas underlying the proposals. The following is not a verbatim account of the scheme; only the main features are dealt with, and that which has a merely local or special importance is excluded.

1. Statistics are compiled as correctly as possible of the country's capital value in plant, buildings, roads, railways, stocks of goods and so on, from sources such as the national budget, and the books of various companies. Both private and public property is included in these statistics, and their values are calculated in current prices.

The aggregate capital value is the basis for the credit which is to be issued. To support this calculation, statistics are also compiled of the goods produced during the previous year, though these are not taken as a limit, since production has not been exploited to its full capacity.

The statistics of the capital value will obviously be only approximate, but will nevertheless form a sufficient basis for the issue of credit, which will correspond only to part of the carefully estimated capital value.

2. On the basis of these statistics a definite yearly sum will be issued to every individual apart from wages or salaries. 1% of the capital value is this is just a total sum to be issued to the population in this way. This sum will be a minimum means of subsistence, and will render superfluous doles, poor relief, pensions, voluntary philanthropic organizations, and the vast expenditure of time and labor which their administration now entails. A considerable amount of time and work will, of course, have to be spent on the administration of this credit issue, but the freedom from investigations such as "means tests" will on the other hand mean the saving of time and friction for both officials and recipients.

This sum may be regarded as a "dividend" accruing to each shareholder in "Great Britain Limited," for example, or in whatever the country in question. It would represent the surplus which every industrialized country has today of stocks of goods and even more potential production. This surplus is due to the work of machines, and to the effort of inventors and workers who have lived in the past, the fruits of which Douglas has called "the cultural heritage of humanity;" if this is to be of any use it must be represented by purchasing power. It must, of course, be understood that Social Credit postulates what is an undisputed fact, viz. potential superabundance. It does not wish to effect a miracle and create something out of nothing, but merely to provide people with purchasing power which will absorb that abundance which is already ours for the asking. The "National Dividend" as it is called, will not be issued for its own sake as a dole to placate the public, but as a necessary technical arrangement to maintain production and distribution at what is now their natural level.

The National Dividend will increase year-by-year as industry becomes more effective, under the impetus afforded by increasing purchasing power. It will not be possible to overdraw it, nor to mortgage it to pay off old debts, public or private, and it will be tax-free.

3. Shares of holding companies and trusts will no longer be privileged (although they will not be forbidden) and no shares with special rights will be acknowledged. Private debt will be recognized and protected so long as it shows itself on inspection to be genuine. Debt to corporations and banks will be examined and partly liquidated with state money.

Buying and selling of real property will no longer be carried out through private persons or institutions (this is to prevent moneylending, executor's sales and more or less compulsory sales). When an owner wishes to give up possession of a property he will apply to the state institution, which will transfer the property to a suitable buyer.

The government will control the financial system but will not administrate any concern, either in agriculture or industry. (Having control of the issue of credit, the state would have an unfair advantage over private competitors.)

4. Control of Prices. This is one of the most important points in the Douglas scheme. The constant gap which now exists between productivity and purchasing power is not due only to the present crisis. It is the inevitable result of the present economic system. Purchasing power is distributed at present through wages, salaries and dividends, and the sum of these can never be sufficient to buy all the goods in existence, for the reason that included in the prices of these goods are items of cost other than wages, salaries and dividends, such as debts, interest, depreciation charges. This is true in the case of any particular undertaking and is therefore true of industry and agriculture has a whole.

Those who hear this argument for the first time usually raise the objection that those costs which are not paid out directly as wages and salaries have actually represented wages and salaries in the previous cycle of production, for instance, in the construction of plant. Up to a point, this is true, as Douglas admits, but costs are never fully covered in this way. For one thing, there is the debt which is directly canceled in the accounts of the bank and which disappears from the money and credit market. Moreover, in a previous cycle of production, the sum of wages, salaries and dividends was here also insufficient to buy what was produced.

In a country, as a whole, therefore, the aggregate of prices is greater than the aggregate of purchasing power. Thus only part of the goods can be bought, and poverty and want in the midst of plenty is the result, or "overproduction" as it is misnamed.

It is difficult to calculate on the average how large the discrepancy really is. In those particular industries of which he has actual knowledge, Douglas says that it is as much as 100%, or even 200%. In a broadcast talk in the autumn of 1934, the late Douglas pioneer, A. R. Orage stated that:

"Our shopkeeper has told us that at a rough estimate our annual output of price values is £10,000 million and probably more. And our taxing officials tell us more accurately that our annual monetary income is about £2,500 million. As four to one, so is our output of price values to the money tickets with which to meet them."

The reason why a breakdown has not come sooner, has been due to the immediate past, according to Douglas, to steadily expanding markets and capital production (which are now becoming restricted) and is due now to bankruptcies, failures and subsidization.

To adjust this disproportion between purchasing power and total prices, Douglas would institute a further measure which he calls the "Just Price," or "Scientific Price Adjustment." Assuming that all prices together represent 100 and all purchasing power, that is to say all incomes, 75, then goods shall be sold to the consumer at three-quarters of the present price of the goods. This would mean that prices would be covered by purchasing power, that everything could be bought. The remaining 25% would be refunded to the producer with state money, and would be equivalent to the capital values, cost of plant, etc. which is responsible for the discrepancy.

The cry goes up "Inflation!" Let us see then what actually happens when prices are reduced by 25%. More can be obtained for money, and hence money becomes more valuable. Prices fall, while at the same time purchasing power increases. Under inflation on the other hand prices rise, and the value of money falls.

Douglas's most recent suggestion is that the 25% should go to the consumer rather than to the producer. The latter would receive the full price for his goods, but the consumer would with every purchase be credited with 25% of the cost price. This would raise purchasing power to the total of prices in the same way as his first scheme but would have the advantage of maintaining the value of money at a more constant level. In any case it will be seen that there is no question of inflation but rather of avoiding deflation. This last plan of a "purchaser's bonus" as it might be called, would stimulate trade considerably, for consumers would be psychologically more inclined to buy if they were offered goods at a discount than if they were offered goods at a reduced price.

By a suitable interchange between the National Dividend and the Just Price production and distribution could be controlled in that degree which was found to be most suitable, for the Just Price would encourage the direct purchase of finished products, while the National Dividend would on the other hand encourage enterprise in industrial undertakings and in agriculture. By increasing the National Dividend at the cost of the Just Price or vice versa either production or consumption could be stimulated, as circumstances demanded.

In the practical example of Silvio Gesell's system which has been previously mentioned–the experiment in Bavaria–distribution was stimulated by the depreciating value of accumulated money–1% per month. In Social Credit, distribution would be stimulated by the offer of a cash "reward" at every purchase. The effect is the same, but a great deal of risk, and many difficulties would be avoided by the Social Credit arrangement which would not necessitate an alteration in the existing kind of money.

It is suggested that the Just Price should be administered in the following manner: The percentage of the cost which must be charged for goods shall be published at certain intervals, just as the discount rate is at present. All recognized businesses shall be registered and shall be supplied with invoice forms which after each purchase shall be filled in, and handed by the customer to his bank, which will credit his account with 25% of the amount of the invoice.

It would not be necessary to constrain legally businesses which refused to cooperate, since they would not be able to issue discount forms, and thus would be faced with 25% subsidized competition. Obviously however, there would have to be serious reasons for such behavior, and safeguards would have to be devised to protect individual organizations from irregular and partisan state interference.

The central bank would refund these proportional discounts to the individual banks. That is to say, the country's capital value would depreciate that amount and "appreciate" with capital development.

This regulation of prices together with Douglas's insistence on the present insufficiency of purchasing power, is one of the most disputed points in Social Credit. A number of writers have endeavored to refute the scheme. Douglas, Adams, Hattersley and others have answered with extensive statistical proofs, in which figures are given for a number of typical industries. These show that there is at present a very big difference between purchasing power and prices. But an even greater difference exists between potential production and present productive output, which is restricted by this lack of purchasing power. As we have already seen, Hattersley and others have calculated that in England productivity could be increased four times, and H. L. Gantt has estimated that in America industry is only 5% effective! Though it is not likely that industry could be made 100% effective, 75%

should be possible, says Hattersley, when one considers actual needs. Hence the mathematical Just Price in England should be 300%. That is to say, 300% additional purchasing power should be added to the present amount to increase the yield of production to the probable demand, i.e. 75% of that output which could, technically speaking, be reached. Such a sudden change would probably cause economic dislocation and difficulties perhaps greater than those from which we now suffer. But when it is suggested that not 300 but 25% should be the initial figure, we realize the care with which the scheme could be instituted. Even such a low figure would considerably ease the working class.

5. Hours of work. The governmental offices acting as models shall inaugurate a working day of four hours and of two shifts, since presumably there would be plenty of work to be done during the first years of Social Credit. There will be no minimum working day or conscription of labor. Such forcible interference with the individual is thought to be more harmful than beneficial and alien to the spirit of Social Credit.

6. Wages. Wages would be paid apart from the National Dividend and as highly as before, and since the amount of work would increase considerably during the first years of Social Credit, the sum of wages would also increase. In the long run, however, since manual work would become less and less, the aggregate of wages would decrease, all the wages for the same unit of work might remain the same, or even increase. On the other hand, the amount of the National Dividend would continually increase and attend more and more to replace switches, as individuals' contribution of work became less in proportion to that machine.

Douglas reckons that in Scotland during the course of the first year under his scheme, the income of a well-paid skilled laborer would increase by between 50 and 100%. For those at present less well situated the increase would of course be proportionately greater, since every individual would receive his National Dividend, assessed at £75 per person for the first year. This dividend would increase year by year as production attained an ever fully capacity through unhampered statistical development, and the individual would become more and more free to devote himself to the arts of leisure.

Meanwhile incomes would be sufficient to allow people to set up decent homes. There would come about the complete revolution in the social morality, and in the conception of the relationship between the state and individual. Up to the present the state has been essentially an authority which has laid claims on the individual which has meted out punishment. On the institution of the National Dividend the state would become a friend, giving material support to each individual born into the world.

But how can the state do this? What has it to give? It has that enormous wealth which our forefathers have created by their toil, their inventiveness and their organization –wealth which is real and concrete. It can't be squandered, or lie unused, but it can also be husbanded for the general benefit. That institution which now expresses our joint interests should naturally take control in this case. This does not mean that the state would own everything but, like an executive servant, would merely issue those tickets which are necessary for the production and distribution of goods and services.

Social Credit would in no way restrict individual enterprise and initiative, since only the control of credit would be in the hands of the state.

Since the state would give, it would also have the right to make conditions. The plan would involve the regulation of wages and profits, within certain limits. We are already acquainted with a certain amount of such legislation, however, and since under Social Credit it would raise incomes to a much higher level without being any more rigid than at present, it would be no cause for complaint.

Employers and others who would not submit to the conditions laid down by the state in this respect, would be free to go their own ways, but would not be able to participate in the benefits which the state had to offer, the National Dividend and the Just Price, since they would be the refusing to observe those conditions which make these benefits possible.

7. Necessity for work. Douglas admits the possibilities of people on the whole would not be inclined to do sufficient work during the first critical period, when they had so much money in their pockets. On the other hand, the immediate results of the scheme would be a huge demand for labor. He suggests therefore that work should be obligatory during the first five years, but that the choice of work should be free. (Obligatory work for a decent wage and at one's own job! That does not sound too bad in this age of unemployment.)

In the case of delinquents there would be no need of trial and imprisonment. If one did not wish to cooperate in the Social Credit community, the National Dividend would be partly or completely withheld.

Such conscription, however, would in all probability be unnecessary. If a man has a yearly income £150 he is hardly likely to refuse work which would bring him in another £150. If he did there might be serious reasons for his behavior, such as the desire to work on a discovery or invention, or to prepare himself for a change in his walk of life, motives which should be respected.

Therein lies the supreme benefit of the National Dividend– the individual's freedom to follow his own bent. To those whose experience in life has given them faith in human nature, it will appear to be the most certain path towards not only an increase in the general happiness, but also towards greater general prosperity.

8. Taxation. There was no longer be any need of direct taxation of the individual or an indirect taxation, such as duties on certain commodities or forms of property, since the state would have control of the source of all money and credit. All that would be necessary would be to withhold a percentage either of the National Dividend or of the Just Price, with which to cover the costs of government.

9. Book-keeping. I will not describe fully here the

accountancy system to be used under Social Credit, details of which have been worked out by certain auditors who support the scheme. Let it suffice to say that in the accounts of the Social Credit state, money (credit) would balance real wealth.

On the basis of this main principle, the details would work themselves out automatically.

What would happen to the nation's currency under Social Credit? is a frequent question. Would not the pound sterling depreciate on the international money market if the scheme were introduced into this country? The answer is the same as in the case of the inflation argument. Social Credit has two possible means of raising purchasing power by price regulation. The one is to lower prices to correspond to purchasing power and to reimburse the producer or retailer with new credit. In this case, the pound would buy more and rise in value, both abroad and at home. So long as the system were enforced only in this country for example, it would attract a number of foreign buyers, which again would probably cause the pound to appreciate still further. The immediate results of this would be favorable, but it would cause considerable irregularities, and perhaps even occasional reprisals. This is one of the reasons why the second suggestion aims at maintaining the prevailing price level and crediting the consumer with the necessary difference. Whether the foreign buyers should receive whole or part of this bonus is a debatable point. Such a bonus would stimulate exports, and would increase the demand for, and the value of, the pound sterling. There would, however, not be so sudden a rise in the value of the pound as when prices were reduced and the producer credited with the difference.

Thus those countries which first introduced Social Credit would have a disproportionate advantage over other countries, but when these followed suit, the relation of values would assume what might be termed a normal character, though unlike that existing now.

Those who argue that Social Credit spells inflation usually do so through a misinterpretation of the scheme, being under the impression that it simply means an increase in the volume of money within the framework of the present system. Actually, it means the issue of just the correct amount of purchasing power to distribute the goods and services available. Inflation, deflation and catastrophic fluctuations in the value of money would be abolished for good.

Another common objection is that the state would not be able to continue to distribute 1% of the capital value of the country year after year as new money, because in 100 years there would be none left. The answer is that the National Dividend would not be entirely new money year after year since part of it would always return to the ordinary channels of commerce either directly, or through the banks, to the National Credit Office in repayment of loans. It would then be reissued as National Dividends, in the same way that limited companies issue dividends year after year. There is no completely new issue of money every year; the money merely circulates.

A certain amount of new money can and should be issued periodically, representing the increase in production during that period. This increase has not been inconsiderable of late years, and it would certainly be far greater under an economic system which did not restrict production. There would be an immediate increase in production not so much on account of increased purchasing power as on account of the security which the promise of the constant purchasing power for the future would afford.

To conclude, Social Credit, unlike Communism, does not imply state ownership of all the means of production and the suppression of individual enterprise, but a state *control* of production, inasmuch as the state would be wholly responsible for the issue of credit.

CHAPTER 8

STABLE MONEY

Stabilized money, as opposed to a currency fixed to gold which other currencies, means one, the value of which is fixed in terms of the average wholesale or retail prices of a definite range of commodities. It does not imply general price regulation or the arbitrary fixing the prices of individual commodities.

Professor Alfred Marshall wrote as far back as 1887 in an article on *Remedies for Fluctuations of General Prices* as follows: "The want of a proper standard of purchasing power is the chief cause of the survival of the monstrous fallacy that there can be too much produced of everything." Professor Irving Fisher, as we have already seen, asserted at the 19th annual Congress of the American Society for Labor Legislation that in his view 19 out of 20 workless could be said to have lost their employment through fluctuations in the value of money.

The demand for a stabilized currency was first heard over 100 years ago. It is perhaps the greatest economic reform movement of the day and there is now every chance that its principles will be put to the test, in view of the vast experiments proceeding in the USA, in Sweden, in Australia, and, to a lesser extent, in England. The movement counts among its supporters many prominent economists, industrial and financiers, for example Irving Fisher, Owen D. Young, Franklin D. Roosevelt in America, J. M. Keynes, Sir Josiah Stamp, the Right Hon. Reginald McKenna, Lord Melchett, Vincent C. Vickers in England, Robert Eisler in Austria, Knute Wicksell, Gustav Cassel, Bertil Ohlin in Sweden, Douglas Copland in Australia, to name only a few. The reformers we have already discussed may be reckoned as being advocates of stable money, especially Silvio Gesell, Arthur Kitson, and Frederick Soddy. In his book, *Stabilized Money*, Professor Fisher refers also to Social Credit as a movement which has persistently pointed to the evil of unstable money values. I for my part am convinced that a stable currency is an essential condition of any sane economic system.

An extraordinarily large number of proposals have been advanced, and several practical experiments have been made, in the name of stabilized money. One of the most prolific and lucid writers on the subject is doubtless Professor Irving Fisher of Yale University. In *Booms and Depressions* (Allen and Unwin, 1933) he sums up the following "Nine Main Factors", the causes of trade cycles, causes which work simultaneously and mutually affect each other. 1. The Debt Factor, 2. The Currency Volume Factor, 3. The Price-Level Factor, 4. The Net-Worth Factor, 5. The Profit Factor, 6. The Production Factor, 7. The Psychological Factor, 8. The Currency-Turnover Factor, 9. Rates of Interest. He then proceeds to show how all these factors vary with variations in the purchasing power of money, and how in his view they could be controlled if this were kept constant. He thereupon puts forward a number of alternative schemes for the attainment of such a constant purchasing power. In some of these the abandonment of the Gold Standard is stipulated, in others its retention. An evolution of the Gold Standard would be the more rational course, he says, but this is by no means necessary and for psychological reasons he thinks it might perhaps be advisable provisionally to retain the Gold Standard. *All those schemes he advances are aimed at affecting for the social good not only the unit of currency but also the means of distribution credit, and the volume of credit.*

It does not lie within the scope of this book to give a detailed description of any of the schemes, which are brilliantly described in the professor's own works. Let it suffice to give you a rough sketch of one particular proposal:

A Bond-Secured Deposit Currency: A plan prepared by James H. Rand Jr., Ragnar Frisch and Irving Fisher

A stabilization commission on behalf of the government sells to banks on demand "Treasury short-term bonds" in proportion to the deposits held by those banks. The banks pay by crediting the government as depositors of a corresponding amount, at, for instance, one year's notice. Interest on both sides cancels itself. Thus the banks obtain increased liquid assets without immediate corresponding increased liabilities, and can increase their outgoing loans in proportion. This procedure would be applied during times of depression. During a boom period the process would be reversed. It is presumed that by such a regulation of credit the purchasing power of money could be kept fairly constant. (This method has been put into practice in a modified form and has been found satisfactory.)

This credit control is limited however by the extent of the gold reserves of which the structure credit is built. The plan must therefore be supplemented by another. Fisher indicates three methods: 1. A marginal store of gold in excess of the necessary reserves, which shall have no function until such time as it is needed for the development of credit. 2. Internationally controlled production of gold. 3. Compensated unit of currency (compensated dollar), that is to say an increase or decrease in the weight of gold behind the currency unit, as the purchasing power of gold in terms of goods increases or decreases.

This leads us to a consideration of President Roosevelt's economic policy. The whole of his experiment is a typical "Stabilized Money" program, with a retention of the Gold Standard. As practical politics this is an innovation, but as an idea it has already been conceived by Professor Alfred Marshall. He was acquainted both with the conception of a "compensated dollar" and "open market operation". Professor Fisher mentions in his book, *Stabilized Money*, that Professor Wilson had before him spoken of a similar procedure– a change of the gold content of the dollar– in this case to avoid inflation.

At the Economic World Conference in London in 1933, two conflicting views were advanced, namely, that of those who wished to stabilize the currencies of individual countries in relation to each other, and that of those, represented by the Roosevelt faction, which sought to stabilize the unit of currency of a country in relation to the purchasing power within that country. Apparently Roosevelt's view was not even understood by many of the delegates present, for if it had been, thinks Professor Fisher, there would have existed the possibility of continued fruitful cooperation. Roosevelt was not alone in advocating at the London Conference a policy of stabilizing the unit of currency in terms of the price level of commodities. A similar proposal came from Austria, represented by Dr. Robert Eisler, and was supported by prominent British financiers. This proposal, which was internationally conceived, will be discussed later in detail.

Roosevelt's policy does not consist only in fixing the purchasing power of the dollar at an arbitrary level but in the first place seeks to attain a level through reflation, which is most just to all classes, especially to the farmers, who have been hardest hit by the depression. In the second place, the problem is to create purchasing power, and later occupation for the mass of unemployed. Apart, therefore, from reflation and a "compensated dollar," a number of other measures have had to be taken: a securing of the credit system through new banking laws, a securing of deposits and the expansion of credit through an increased volume of currency notes and through low rates of interest for the execution of public works, etc. Then came the great task for common agreement within industry, with a view to increased private enterprise and if possible higher wages.

As further measures for the stabilization of the dollar came *The Gold Reserve Act of 1934* which transferred all gold to the government and which gives for the time being supreme power to the President and to the Secretary of the Treasury to manage the currency (Fisher, *Stabilized Money*) and *The Silver Purchase Act of 1934* which incorporated silver as a basis of money.

Roosevelt's policy has met with so much resistance and

so many difficulties that people are apt to have strong doubts as to its outcome. However, it must not be thought that all possible paths has been explored. Those who are familiar with the possibilities of economic politics would rather say that the USA has only just made a start. In *Stabilized Money*, Fisher gives us a sincere and very welcome insight into his own hopes for the future, which are of special interest in that he is a great influence in present-day American politics. He writes:

"As soon as politically feasible, I would go even further along the line of Senator Cutting's bill. I would have the government practically take away from the banks the entire function of creating and destroying circulating medium, leaving to the banks the strictly banking functions such as lending money. This project, now favored by many economists, particularly Simons and others at the University of Chicago, and by some bankers, such as George le Blanc, is the subject of a book I am writing called *The 100% System of Money and Banking*. Under this system *all checking accounts would have behind them a reserve of lawful money of 100%*. [Author's italics.] An incidental, but at the same time, a very great advantage of this system would be that it would reduce *the government debt*, now reaching alarming proportions. It would do this by *substituting non-interest-bearing obligations for interest-bearing obligations*, up to the point needed to restore and to maintain a stable price level."

While Roosevelt in America was launching his colossal experiment and the direction of stabilized money with the retention of the Gold Standard, there was already in full swing in Sweden another big stabilization experiment without the retention of the Gold Standard, an extremely successful one, which Fisher considers the most remarkable one in the history of money.

When in September 1931, England went off gold, Sweden followed suit after an interval of one week. Inflation, and a fall in the value of currency was then feared. Thereupon the Riksbank announced that it is intended to try to maintain a constant purchasing power of money in consumers' hands. As a basis, the price index for ordinary commodities and services in 15 different districts was worked out. The index basis, and the importance attached to the different commodities are constantly revised in relation to the changing demands. The Riksbank also takes into consideration other indexes such as wholesale price index, production index, trade index, and unemployment index. By manipulating the discount rate, by buying and selling gold, government bonds and foreign money the Riksbank has, according to statements published at the end of 1934 and the beginning of 1935, succeeded in maintaining the purchasing power of money constant in terms of the retail price index within a maximum variation of 1 3/4 percent. (Living maximum 101.7 and minimum 98.4.)

Australia countered the crisis from 1929 onwards by measures similar to those taken in the USA. In the summer of 1931 the value of money was depreciated by "raising the price of gold" and the credit of the central bank was simultaneously expanded. Thus the fall in export prices was met by reducing inland costs and debts in accordance with a tabular standard. The success of these measures is described by Professor Douglas Copland in his book, *Australia in the World Crisis,* and by Irving Fisher in his *Stabilized Money.*

Of the United Kingdom and the "Sterlingaria" countries (that is those countries which kept their monies at exchange parity with the English pounds, after England had left the Gold Standard in September 1931) Professor Fisher writes: "The majority of this group signed a so-called *Imperial Declaration,* which said that a continued rise in commodity prices was most desirable in order to restore the activity of industry and employment, ensure an economic return to the producer of primary commodities, and harmonize the burden of debt and fixed charges with economic capacity." This position was not very different from Mr. Roosevelt's.

Fisher's point of view is supported by some of the most prominent English financial authorities, among whom we quote the following:

J. M. Keynes in the *New York Herald Tribune,* July 4, 1933, writes: "The President's message –is in substance a challenge to us to decide whether we propose to tread the old unfortunate ways or to explore new paths, paths new to statesmen and to bankers, but not new to thought. For they lead to the managed currency of the future, the examination of which has been the prime topic of postwar economics."

Sir Josiah Stamp in *Spectator*, November 1928: "What about trade depression in the basic industries, unemployment, labor unrest, class hatred, high taxation, and the rest? My answer is that the problem of the price level is fundamental to a solution of them all."

Reginald McKenna in *Midland Bank Monthly Review*, August-September 1933: "The proposed declarations (of the gold block) would have tied the world to the wrong end of the stick... He (President Roosevelt) at least, was for seizing the right end ..."

The situation in the world today is, therefore, that one country, Sweden, has introduced stabilized money. In the USA and Australia it will be introduced as soon as an appropriate price level is maintained through reflation. The United Kingdom and the "Sterlingaria" countries have not definitely pledged themselves to stabilization but they are pursuing a policy of reflation milder in form than that of the USA and there are indications that this group will in due course also adopt stabilization. Stabilized money, therefore, is now on the point of being put into practice by the leading financial countries of the world.

DR. ROBERT EISLER

The Austrian, Dr. Eisler, is one of the most prominent contemporary historians, and he has specialized in the history of money. He has been engaged by the League of Nations and has written several treatises on historical and practical financial questions. We will here consider only the proposal which he submitted to the World Economic Conference, and which is to be found in his work *Stable Money—The Remedy for the Economic World Crisis*. What characterizes Eisler, apart from his faith in stable money, is his realization of the vast productive powers of the world today and so great a belief in the possibility of exploiting them, that his proposal has more the stamp of a gigantic plan of the industrial expansion than of a stabilization project.

In a forward to *Stable Money*, Mr. Vincent C. Vickers, a former Director of that fortress of orthodox finance, the Bank of England, writes as follows: "Whether or not I, a former Director of the Bank of England, am qualified to judge, to endorse or to condemn opinions on the past, present and future monetary policies of this country and the world, may be a debatable point! But I am fully qualified to tell the public that, in my view, it is entirely mistaken if it believes that the monetary system of this country is normally managed by 'recognized monetary experts' working in accordance with the most scientific and up-to-date methods known to modern economists.

"From a purely national point of view, it is necessary to realize how extremely important it is that the Bank of England should no longer attempt to stifle the efforts of modern economists, nor persist in regarding all 'Money Reformers' as impertinent busybodies trying to usurp her authority. As long as things go well, or are thought to be going well, such procedure is entirely as it should be... but when things go wrong, terribly wrong! When we are told one day that the national safety depends upon adherence to the Gold Standard no matter what the sacrifice! And a week or so later that our abandonment of it will bring salvation and prosperity to our industries! When the pulling of old levers no longer moves the signals! When the patient no longer responds to the old prescriptions! When we see great sections of the community clamoring for monetary reform,—then, surely, it is time for the government to seek advice elsewhere, and to encourage open discussion...

"... it is not 'productive industry' with this new machinery, which is the root cause of our unemployment and our uncertainty, but 'finance' with its antiquated mechanism, which has failed to adapt itself to modern requirements..."

In his own preface Dr. Eisler names the 72 prominent

economists, politicians and industrialists with whom he has exchanged his views. He mentions these names "in order that the scheme of monetary reform here put forward may not be dismissed as a visionary paper project of an isolated theoretician."

Dr. Eisler aims at an international scheme of industrial expansion backed by a corresponding expansion of the volume of money and credit.

The peculiarities of the plan are, in the first place, the method by which it is hoped to avoid, or circumvent, a rise in prices in individual countries and, in the second place the international aspect of the scheme.

The first peculiarity, viz. the method of avoiding the evil effects of rising prices, is expounded in the chapter on "Compensating the Effects of Inflation on the Cost of Living" as follows: "If new money is put into circulation, as it must be by means of the payroll either of large-scale public works, or equally important private enterprise, i.e. through the building and engineering trades, a vast amount of wages is paid out for a certain time without anything being added to the existing stock of directly consumable goods. In this way the existing disproportion between supply and demand is corrected and the glut of consumable goods relieved. But however desirable this may be, the resulting rise of the general price level, exaggerated through speculation, will immediately deprive all those who have fixed monetary incomes (rentiers, annuitants, officials, etc. as well as the already employed and the newly re-engaged workers) of a certain part of their real income. This typical consequence of all credit expansions or currency inflations cannot in the least be avoided by the proposed international generalization and by the exact synchronization and proportionalization of the additional expenditure in all countries. It has nothing whatever to do with the foreign exchanges of a country and could not be avoided by pegging them.... Yet, in spite of the cheapening of production through the enlarged turnover of the producers, and the consequent reduction of the per-unit proportion of overhead and social charges, and in spite of the actually existing glut of finished goods of all kinds, it is evident that the supplementary purchase-power created by the circulation of additional currency that immediately raised the retail price level of all commodities. (The additional currency very soon reaches the vaults of the banks and creates 10 and 11 times as much new deposits because the banks try to maintain the customary ratio between deposits and cash in hand.) The boom would be started by speculators– as is always the case under similar circumstances– even before the expansion of the monetary circulation has set in; and it would be accentuated by every official move towards the new monetary policy.

"Such a boom would, in the first instance, be beneficial and necessary, in order to stop the present falling tendency of wholesale prices. [This was written in 1932 – author.] it would overcome by means of speculative anticipation of the proposed international financial action, the lethargic stagnation of the great world markets. It is the speculative boom which would at once cut short the indecision of all buyers who are now lying low and awaiting a further slump in prices. Their sudden panic buying would quickly liquidate the frozen stocks of merchants and manufacturers and the emptied stores would encourage the sending out of new orders to the producers. The manufacturers would in turn increase their production and easily finance this increase through new bank credits, which would readily be granted to them as soon as they could point out that their sales had started anew.

"The mere psychological turn of the tide would be sufficient to make available to industry and agriculture the considerable amount of currency which is actually being hoarded or offered in profusion in the short term loan market, as well as the large volume of bank credits created by the commercial banks whenever they think that such loans can be profitably used by their clients. To this anticipatory speculative movement the quantity of real currency which would have to be issued in order to re-enlist all unemployed would probably not exceed a small part of the present volume of money in circulation, especially since the expense of the initial increase in all wages and salaries, adjusting them at some point to the rise in price level, can easily be met out of the funds which are now contributed by the state, by the employer and by the workers, towards the cost of unemployed relief.

"The boom could not, however, go on indefinitely. In spite of the increased public expenditure and the increased nominal income of the salaried class and in spite of the cheapening of mass production through increased turnover, the real income of all individuals, except for the entrepreneur and the intelligent intermediary, and therefore the total consumers' purchase power would again decline after a lapse of time."

After a lengthy explanation of how purchase power would move from wage earners and rentiers to shareholders and entrepreneurs, Dr. Eisler continues:

"The present writer himself would condemn any scheme of monetary reorganization which began by raising the purchase power of one group at the expense of another.

"Fortunately the proper method for avoiding this and for counteracting automatically and continually the above enumerated evils of inflation is quite well known ever since, in 1847, Massachusetts Bay Colony introduced a simple tabular standard based on the prices of wheat, meat, leather, and wool in order to compensate the effects of the inflation of the 'Colonial Notes' circulation on the revenues of its creditors, officers and soldiers.

"Nothing is necessary but the introduction of a new, very simple monetary law in all countries willing to participate in the proposed currency expansion scheme—a law extending the well-known principle of index wages to all existing contracts in terms of money.

"This legislation would provide that every monetary obligation in force at a given date—all contracts concerning wages, salaries and appointments, all laws fixing taxes, rights and duties, all stipulations concerning insurances, bank deposits or credits, loans or mortgages, rent or interest, all deeds of sale, all commercial bills etc. should be carried out with due regard to the actual purchasing power of the national money at the time when the payment stipulations is effected, the temporary purchasing power of the money being ascertained by means of index numbers representing the average retail price have a fair number of consumable goods, the cost of rents, rates, taxes, local transport, and the elementary education at that particular moment in terms of the appropriate monetary unit. Such legislation would be tantamount to redefining the monetary unit of the UK or of the USA in case of their joining the proposed monetary federation. The following is a tentative draft of the proposed law:

"1. The monetary unit is the currency of the UK (USA) is the pound sterling (USA dollar).

"2. The pound sterling (USA dollar) is the Bank of England (Federal Reserve Bank) note which was equivalent to 122.24719 grains (23.22 grains) of fine gold at the London gold price of 18 September, 1931.

"3. The pound sterling (USA dollar) note is legal tender to the extent of its actual purchasing power.

"4. The term 'actual purchasing power' is defined as the reciprocal value of the cost of living index obtaining on the day of payment.

"5. The cost of living index is calculated on the basis of the average cost of the following commodities: ..., of local transport, of rents, taxes and rates, and other expenses for elementary education.

"Through such a law for two functions of money–its use as a medium of exchange (legal tender) and its use as a means of accumulating capital (deferred purchasing power) or contractual income for the future–would henceforward be separated more completely than now.

"Under the new system that would be two sorts of money: 1. legal tender, call the pound or USA dollar of 'current money' or money proper (£ cr. or $ cr.) and 2. banker contract money of account, called a pound or dollar *banco* (£bo or $bo). Money *banco* would be obtained by concluding a contract about a future payment of money proper or by depositing 'current money' with the bank or similar institution. Current money would be exclusively used for small transactions between persons not well known to each other or not in possession of a bank account, especially for the payment of wages, transport fares and occasional retail purchases. All of the payments would be effected by means of bank money, that is by checks or travelers cheques or transfers of money *banco*. All prices in catalogs of shops selling goods of which the price does not vary much, (e.g. books, clothes, jewelry, cigars, tobacco, wines) would be marked in money *banco*. The index multiplicator of the week would be affixed to the desk of the cashier who would calculate by means of simple multiplication or conversion tables published in the Sunday papers the sums due in 'current money'.

"This was how retail business, inn and hotel keeping was done in Germany at the height of the inflation in 1923, when the 'stable mark' was introduced as a money of accounts alongside the paper mark used as current money.

"All bank and business accounts would, however, be calculated without any additional complication in money *banco*, current money being exchanged against bank money by special letters only in so far and as soon as a client wanted to pay in or draw out current money.

"Mr. Alec Wilson has suggested a simple, and perhaps to Englishmen, a more acceptable way of distinguishing the unit of current money from the unit of 'money of account'. The British public is quite accustomed, ever since the memorable 21st September, 1931, to seeing in the popular papers how many shillings the pound is worth on a given day. In these most misleading statements, which are intended to keep alive 'the gold mentality of the masses', the equation between the pound and so many shillings is meant to tell the reader how many hypothetical 'gold shillings' an inconvertible paper pound would buy in London, Paris or New York.

"In an analogous, but more realistic way we might henceforward decide to call the units of current money– the medium of exchange for petty trade and for paying out wages – 'shillings' and 'pence' as usual, or 'shillings' and 'pence *cash*', reserving the term pound or 'pound cheque' for the unit of bank money used for all the more important transactions.

"Current money will, of course, slowly but constantly depreciate through the expansion of credit and currency necessary to meet the requirements of increasing production and consumption, the rate of increase being no longer limited except for the necessity of expanding the expenses of the various countries into proportion to their actual spending power as measured by the volume of their present Gold Standard currencies and by the physical limits of production. This will naturally force commercial and clearing banks to diminish as far as possible their cash reserves by increasing their balances at the national banks, and all private people to spend or deposit current money as quickly as possible. In this way the circuit philosophy of currency which is now one of the most intractable factors of monetary instability, will always be maintained at its maximum value, i.e. stabilized as far as possible and the maximum available credit will be automatically placed at the disposition of traders and producers.

"The power of bank money to purchase consumable goods would be absolutely constant, even in periods of credit or currency expansion.

"Wages and salaries, interest and rent being fixed in bank money, i.e. subject by statute to regular increase corresponding to an eventual rise in index figures, the (nominally) rising price level will in no way diminish the real wages of the manual and intellectual worker or the income of the rentier, nor will it increase the wages bill of the employer. Conversely, the real cheapening of production through the increase of output and proportionate diminution of overhead charges made possible by increased consumption will accrue in the shape of higher profits to the entrepreneur, so that he will be able to spend or re-invest on a larger scale and thus create further opportunities for employee labor in the production of new capital goods and intellectual trades.

"In terms of this bank money the price of each individual commodity or service will vary as before in relation to the average price of all commodities. But this average – the so-called retail price level of consumable goods–is practically stabilized within very narrow limits, that is to say it can only vary during the interval between the publication of two successive cost-of-living indices. Since the cost of living index is a retail price index based on figures which move much more slowly than the 'reagible' wholesale prices, the movements which are possible between successive index calculations based on the market prices of each Saturday–the day following the Friday evening wage payments in current money or in wage cheques– are practically negligible.

"Readers who remember the vertiginous price movement in German, Austrian and Polish retail markets in the heyday of inflation may be inclined to imagine that equally rapid price movements would take place under the influence of the compensated currency expansion. They forget that these price movements were caused by the demand for commodities which was artificially stimulated because people were prevented from converting current into stable money, that is, into claims on stable purchase power."

There follows a statistical account of rising prices during a typical inflationary period. He shows that the rise is at first gradual and that violent rises only come in the later phases. He continues:

"If the slow and unimportant initial depreciation of current money is compensated from the start by the facility of converting current money *either* into commodities or into stable bank money, it is highly probable that the movement of nominal prices will be slow or rather regular. *If the contrary should happen through the panicky reaction of the people who remember the days of former inflations, it would not matter* [author's italics], because the only untoward consequence of the rapid depreciation of current money would be the need to publish biweekly or even daily index figures for a short time until the public got accustomed to the new mechanism.

"On first consideration, the expert reader will be inclined to object that the use of a money of account alongside current money is not a new invention, and that all previous attempts to introduce such a double standard have been failures, as is proved by the fact that it has always disappeared after a short time. At the height of inflation in 1923, Germany tried to introduce a money of account, variously called *Festmark* or 'gold-mark' and attached to the US dollar. In a similar way, Poland had in 1922 its Zloty, which was at first nothing but a money-of-account equivalent to the Swiss franc.

"Quite recently (14th of August, 1931), Hungary has introduced in view of the beginning of the depreciation of its 'pengo' notes a theoretical 'gold pengo' to service standard of all private and public monetary contracts and obligations: in this way it was hoped to maintain Hungarian gold prices and contractual obligations on a *par* with those in Gold Standard countries. *All these various monies in account were and are, however, entirely dependent on the variable purchase power of gold and quite independent of the commodity price level of the country.*" [Author's italics.)

The above will have given an impression of the scheme from the national point of view. Before proceeding to a consideration of the international aspects, mention should be made of some objections which are commonly made to Eisler's principles.

It is often claimed that prices would rise in direct proportion to the increase of credits and that there would, therefore, be no real expansion of purchasing power. Eisler's statistics of typical inflationary periods show, however, that the rise in prices is not at first proportionate to an increased volume of money and credit but only later assumes such a direct relationship. With Eisler's scheme a controlling factor would from the start hinder any such violent rising prices. Moreover it is not always certain the prices rise with increasing credits and increasing industrial activity. Many unforeseen contingencies may arise. Experience of ordinary inflationary periods has at all events shown that these in the long run actually do create an increased purchasing power and apart from slump periods, purchasing power has steadily increased during the last hundred years. It would, therefore, appear likely that if the regulating mechanism existed, this increase might proceed evenly, without catastrophic interruptions. Eisler's scheme implies such a regulating mechanism.

Others maintain that the small trader who buys at a wholesale price and sells at a fixed retail price will suffer through Eisler's system in that "wholesale prices would at first be constantly on the increase while retail prices would be kept constant." But it should be sufficiently obvious that wholesale prices cannot constantly rise while retail prices are kept at a fixed level. Wholesale prices will as usual react to other and greater fluctuations than retail prices but the very fact that retail prices are constant will make the risk of fluctuations in wholesale prices less than under a completely uncontrolled inflationary period. Thus, those who ask how the rise in wholesale prices is to be checked are putting the cart before the horse. Retail prices must necessarily react on wholesale prices and thus on the whole productive apparatus. This introduces us to another aspect of the question.

A number of critics stress the fact that the proposal attached importance to consumers' income and they recall that it is in the heavy industries and not in the consumable goods industries that a crisis as a rule starts. An intelligent study of Eisler's proposal will show, however, that it is on this very fact that he builds. The whole of his plan starts with the assumption that expanded credit will directly benefit heavy industries and public works, but that the consumer must at the same time be protected against a rise in prices. As expanded credit benefits heavy industry the increased production here will also counteract the rise in wholesale prices.

Regarding the international aspect of the question Eisler writes: "The maintenance of legal index wages and salaries in one country is of course impossible beyond the limits set by the competition of other countries. *Index wages cannot be maintained nationally*, with the exception of those in the so-called sheltered industries. And the other industries' basic gold wages must be reduced under the pressure of foreign competition. In other words, there is no way stabilizing *nationally* the retail price level or reciprocally the purchase power of a *national* money.

"While it is obvious that a national, as well as an international, money of account based on the gold parity relation is incapable of stabilizing the general price level nationally or internationally, this is not at first sight so clear in the case of the *national* money-of-account based on a tabular commodity standard of the type of the primitive system applied in 18th century Massachusetts. The system was tried in Russia in 1922 in the form of the so-called 'goods rouble', only to be abandoned very soon in favor of gold claim currency (the tchernovcy or 'goulden' notes). The explanation, in this case is very simple. In order to finance a country's imports, accumulated claims in national money must be exchangeable without loss into monetary claims in foreign countries. Since the fixed quantity of commodities and services linked to a national claim based on his tabular standard at a constant retail price cannot itself be freely transferred like gold into another country, such a claim must be convertible into a freely and cheaply transportable quantity of gold or gold exchange, or into a foreign warehousing warrant for which an equal quantity of goods and services can be obtained at a fixed wholesale price in other countries. If this is not the case, such claim will be offered abroad for what it will fetch. The price in terms of gold or gold exchange or foreign goods warrants which the seller will be able to obtain such a claim will fall with the growing value of the imports needed by a country and with the diminishing quantity of its exports. As soon as the foreign exchange value of such a claim has fallen below par, it will not be exchanged against gold claims, but at a discount, even within the country itself. On the other hand, increased exports will diminish the quantity of goods offered on the home markets and thus raise several *banco* prices of all commodities. This will of course destroy the inherent essential stability of the purchase power of a monetary claim based on the national cost-of-living index. The internal purchase power of such a claim will on the last instance depend on the quantity of purchase power *in gold or gold exchange standard* countries, against which it can't be exchanged at home or abroad at a given moment.

"The first condition for the stabilization of the general price level of the national purchase power currency is the *international stabilization of the exchanges* through the parallel, proportionate and synchronic development of production and consumption in the various countries *by means of proportional supplementary budgets and the preliminary exchange of mutual stabilization credits.* If these indispensable conditions are realized by international treaty, *the simultaneous application of the tabular standard in each country is the necessary complement of the measures stated.*" (An agreement among a certain group of countries would suffice. The cooperation of every country would not be necessary. This point will be dealt with later.)

"Since these conditions have never before been realized the failure of all previous experiments with indexed currencies cannot be used as an argument against the possibility of organizing an expansible currency of monetary units with stable purchase power by means of a logical coordination of the three above explained measures.

"Another *prima facie* objection to the proposed system is based on the fact that the cost of living is naturally very different in the various countries which might wish to participate in such a monetary reorganization. The obvious answer is that equally so, within each country, the cost of living differs in various cities, towns and villages. In Germany, officials are paid varying local supplements to their wages, according to whether they have to live in the capital or in a cheap provincial town. Nobody would expect the difference in the local purchase power of money having any other effect, but that impoverished rentiers occasionally migrate from Berlin to Pasewalk.

"The cost-of-living variation cannot cause any exchange fluctuations in the proposed system, since international trade is carried on exclusively by means of bank money. Experience has shown moreover that in countries with pegged exchanges, like Egypt and the UK, the national price levels will rise and fall together." J. M. Keynes has dealt with this question in *A Treatise on Money*.

I will here explain why and how the exchanges within the group of countries should according to Dr. Eisler be "pegged."

There is nothing to prevent a proportional increase of credit and money circulation in all the countries taking part in this game since everywhere there is need of increased circulation. But when we come to the question of what use to which this credit shall be put in private and public works, increased wages and pensions, etc. we are faced with a difficulty. It would be practically impossible to calculate the relative effects of, for example, flood control works on the Mississippi, electrification of English railways and the construction of a dam on the Seine. The different consequences of these operations on the exchanges of the countries involved in the scheme will induce fluctuations which might jeopardize its success, especially when these fluctuations are aggravated by speculation. To guard against this contingency, therefore, "stabilization credit" will be needed from the start with which to "peg" the exchanges.

During the war, for instance, the currencies of the Allied countries were bound together in this way. With the help of credit reserves in New York, the Anglo-American, the Franco-British and the Italiano-French exchanges were stabilized up to 1919 with the result that it was possible to buy, at fixed rates, liras in Paris, francs in London and pounds in New York. Since during the war the European powers in the main consumed what America produced, the necessity of stabilization was occasioned by a one-sided economic relationship, which found its expression in the War Debt. It would be otherwise if a similar apparatus were set up between a number of countries for simultaneous effort to conquer unemployment. Stabilization credits would be exchanged between all these nations in relation to the conditions of money circulation existing in each. Stabilization would be reciprocal and, in general, would not create a one-sided indebtedness of one to the other.

This stabilization plan is by no means a new and fantastic invention. It has worked admirably in a simple form between England and Egypt since 1916 and in a yet more modified form between England and the Malay states, Nigeria, the Gold Coast and Sierra Leone. It was on account of the difficulty of shipping gold between England and Egypt during the war that the bank of Egypt was empowered in 1916 to issue each Egyptian pound notes on the security of British government bonds. Anglo-Egyptian exchange has been constant ever since at 97 1/2piastres to the pound. Dr. D. W. Shaw describes the process in *Currency, Credit and the Exchanges*. A Londoner buying a draft for £100,000 on Alexandria hands the sum to Egypt's National Bank in London and the receiver of the draft obtains from the bank in Egypt 97,437,500 pilasters. Currency notes representing the sum are then added to the volume of money in circulation and the Egyptian guarantee fund in London is increased by £100,000, of which the greater part is invested in British treasury bills, only a small amount is retained for daily requirements on account in the bank of England. The procedure is reversed equally simply, the volume of money being reduced in Egypt and the guarantee reduced in London by the sale of securities.

The key to this mechanism lies in those values or securities which are deposited in London against the issue of notes in Cairo and vice versa. *Such a system practically speaking unites the monetary systems of two countries* and makes money transactions between those countries as simple as money transactions within a country. The Anglo-Egyptian arrangement works equally well in periods of inflation or deflation.

It is such a system that Eisler suggests should be adopted between all entities of the British Empire and certain other European countries, which together would form a "self-supporting" organization.

This group would be very fortunately placed with regard to War Debts since the total gold production of the British Empire would alone be more than sufficient to cover the interest on, at a small percentage amortization of, the War Debts.

Eisler thinks that if so large and suitable a unit as the British Empire with its natural complement of a few other nations does not come to such an arrangement in the near future, a smaller group as for example the Central Powers will have to do it, for the protection of their vital interests. Such a group will not be able to settle its War Debts with its gold output and will have deliberately to declare itself bankrupt to the creditor nations outside the group and also to a certain extent break off trade connections with those nations, and live as best it can on its own resources–a procedure which would be in the highest degree detrimental to the creditor nations.

This is one of the reasons why Eisler is so much in favor of an adoption of his plan by the British Empire in conjunction with the Scandinavian countries, Portugal and a few others.

On the basis of his principles, Dr. Eisler has made the following *Tentative Draft of an International Agreement on Monetary Policy.*

"For the purpose of stabilizing both internationally and nationally the purchase power of their various currencies the High Contracting Parties hereafter called the member nations of the International Monetary Federation agree to take the following measures:

"1. The federated governments undertake to exchange each with each other equivalent amount of specially issued regularly renewable Treasury Bills (Federal Reserve Bills) corresponding in volume to the average money value of one year's trade between the two member nations. These bills will be signed by the Treasury of the issuing and accepted by the Treasury of the receiving country, the equivalence being calculated on the basis of the parity of exchange henceforth to be kept invariable by the sale and purchase of the said Federal Reserve Bills.

"2. The federated governments undertake to expand the respective monetary circulations *pari passu* and in equal proportion to the actual volume of their national notes issue and their Central Bank's sight liabilities.

"3. The said expansion credits will be used by the federal nations for the purpose of balancing existing budget deficits, restoring recent cuts in the salaries of state and communal officials, in old age pensions, in unemployment benefits, etc., for reducing the burden of direct and indirect taxation and increasing government and local expenditure on public works, national and international capital development, as well as for the purpose of granting cheap credit to private enterprise.

"4. The High Contracting Parties undertake not to use any part of the newly created credits for the purpose of additional armaments.

"5. In order to protect the owners of the fixed monetary incomes, especially the wage and salary earners, against the inevitable consequences of monetary depreciation concomitant with the proposed expansion of individual national monetary circulations, the federated governments undertake to alter the monetary loss of their countries in such a way as to declare the circulating money (banknotes and divisionary coin) legal tender to the extent of the purchase power of the monetary unit on the day of payment, this purchase power to be determined as the reciprocal value of a suitably constructed cost-of-living index.

"6. In order to stabilize the purchase power of bank or contract-money of account in terms of commodities the High Contracting Parties undertake to incorporate in the statutes of their respective National Banks the obligation for the said Banks of Issue to control credit by means of the discount rate and eventual open market operations in such a way as to keep wholesale prices of all commodities entering into international trade as stable as possible at the optimal level ensuring the fullest employment of capital and labor in the federated countries.

"7. For the purpose of furthering the international cooperation of the various National Banks, their governors or deputy governors will assemble in conference once a month at the seat of the B.I.S. in Bâle to discuss and frame the necessary measures.

"8. Within the limits of this agreement, stipulating a parallel and proportional expansion of the member nations' budgets and monetary situations, the federated governments and their National Banks will preserve their entire liberty of action as before.

"9. The federated National Banks undertake to buy gold and silver in any quantity at the minimum prices of— pounds an ounce fine of gold and — pounds an ounce fine of silver and to sell warrants for any quantity superior in value to £20,000 of both metals at the London market price of the day. They will not under any conditions whatever hinder by embargoes, taxes, stamp or other duties or in any other way the free exports and imports of the two precious metals.

"10. The High Contracting Parties undertake to ratify within a month after the signature of this agreement the Geneva Convention concerning the eight hours working day, and to convene within a month from this day a conference of experts in order to discuss the possibility of introducing the five days week and the total suppression of child labor at the earliest possible date.

"11. This agreement shall be valid from the day of its ratification by all the member nations of the Federation until 12 months after due notice has been given by any member who wishes to resign membership of the Federation.

"12. All differences concerning the interpretation of this agreement shall be settled by a Committee of Arbitration nominated by the League of Nations Secretary-General, subject to an appeal to the Hague Court. Pending the appeal the member nation shall conform to the decision of the Arbitration Committee.

CHAPTER 9

SOME NORWEGIAN "NEW ECONOMISTS"

I n Norway there is a very real appreciation of our present economic problems and in the following pages I shall describe a few proposals made by Norwegian writers of the new schools of economic thought.

Professor Ragnar Frisch, in a pamphlet titled *Sparing og Cirkulasjonsregulering (Saving and the Control of Circulation)* has advanced a solution of the economic depression, which has much in common with the proposals of Eisler, Douglas and Soddy. He refers therein to the German "Notverordnung" of September 1932, through which the economic life of the country was relieved by considerable remissions of taxation. The government abandoned the idea of balancing the budget until more prosperous times and Professor Frisch suggest that such a method of financial regulation might be adopted to advantage by any state as a fixed policy. Similar to *A Bond-Secured Deposit Currency* h.89.

The following extract from the Professor's pamphlet will be seen to be a clear argument for a number of "new economic" views, notably for the Douglas scheme for direct issue of credit to the consumer:

"With regard to the possibility of achieving a solutions for monetary measures postwar experience has shown that, contrary to the belief we held, it is not possible to regulate the productive activities of the community merely by manipulating the discount rate. An equal lack of success has attended the efforts of certain central banks to supplement the effect of the discount rate by such measures as the "Open

Market Operations" instituted in America by the Federal Reserve system. Not even have such organizations as the Reconstruction Finance Corporation shown themselves able to bring any effective stimulus to production.

"This does not imply that all monetary measures must be doomed from the outset. There is a definite reason for the failure of the above-named measures and this can doubtless be found in the difference which exists between what might be called the *sales* crisis and the *liquidity* crisis. The fault of these American and similar schemes in other countries is that they have concentrated exclusively on the latter. Resources have been placed at the disposition of banks but nothing has been done directly to promote sales. It was hoped that the first result of more abundant credit would be to stimulate production and that a sufficiency of purchasing power would by this means percolate through to the hands of workers, executives and other consumers.

"Such was not the case. The maladjustment in the distribution of purchasing power is now such that it cannot be righted by this means. Most industrialists now consider with reason that they are not justified in increasing production without first having proof that demand will be more normal. Even concerns with the large liquid capital therefore lie low. They place their capital rather by passive than by active investment. Others, who have courage and initiative but limited resources find themselves baulked.

"Thus we get that paradoxical situation characteristic of a certain stage in a depression: the banks are relatively well supplied with means but nevertheless restrict loans because they find that would be borrowers are not sufficiently "sound". But it is precisely on account of the trade depression that they are not "sound" and neither will they be unless trade improves.

"This explains why those measures which have aimed only at solving the monetary crisis have come to nought. The inference is that more rational plans which take into account both the trade crisis and the monetary crisis would be more likely to achieve some success..."

In a later proposal Professor Frisch suggests the institution of a clearing center or "National Exchange Service", where goods and services could be bartered, independently of money. Recourse to its help would be voluntary and it would not supplant but merely supplement the existing money system, at least in its initial stages.

The professor has explained the principles of his exchange service in *Econometrica*, the Journal of the Econometric Society of Colorado USA Volume 2, numbers 1 and 4, July and October 1934, in an article entitled *Distributive Planning: Proposal for a National Organization of a Commodity and Service Exchange*. The article opens with a short survey of present conditions and of the reasons for the breakdown of the distributive system. There follows a detailed description of the proposed exchange service. Producers would submit reports of what goods they would need during a prescribed period, assuming that a certain sale of their own products were guaranteed. At the same time statistics of how much could be produced would be collected, and from the information obtained a plan of production and distribution would be evolved. To illustrate the scope and purpose of the scheme and the Professor's faith in it the conclusion of the article is here given:

"1. The Organization of a National Exchange service for a country seems, both on theoretical and practical grounds, to be possible. There can scarcely be any doubt such an arrangement would help greatly to *break through* the obstacles of a purely distributive kind which the depression has created. Pessimism and lack of confidence would not be able to stop the exchange within such a system inasmuch as the participants would be placed face-to-face with the *fait accompli* that they have those things which will enable them to buy the goods they want. They would not first have to obtain the means by increase sale of their own products. The vicious phase connection between sales and purchases would be broken.

"2. The arrangement involves practically no financial responsibility for the State. The State's expenses will only be for administration and to cover losses caused by direct frauds.

"3. The arrangement is enormously *elastic*. According to the desires of the participants, the volume of the exchange may be increased or decreased, or, if the case arises, may be diverted in new directions, without necessitating any great alteration in the administration and the technical apparatus.

"4. If the system gradually works itself in, one will thereby obtain a real *survey* of the forces that exist both on the demand and supply side in economic life."

A far more radical scheme is to be found in a book by Thorolf Winter-Hjelm, *Kapitalrente og ågerrente*, 1930 (*Capital Interest and Usury*). Winter-Hjelm's plan is closely related to that of the Free Economists. He also suggests the use of money having a limited period of circulation (one year) but which, unlike that of the Free Economists, would not depreciate gradually nor require a troublesome application of stamps. Instead, a small fee would be charged on exchanging the old currency for the new. There would be a "winding-up period" during the first three months of the year. This procedure makes the plan more practicable than that of the Free Economists. Winter-Hjelm's plan is of special interest in that he considers it possible, in common with Douglas and Silvio Gesell, but as opposed to Eisler, to introduce the managed money and credit system within a single country without the support afforded by international currency cooperation.

Mr. O. H. Medbøe, founder and for many years managing chairman of two of Norway's banks, in 1934 published plans in the form of a series of lectures for a new economic and administrative system. Among other things he suggests that the function of the Norwegian central bank be limited to the supervision of foreign transactions, for which the present currency and its relation to gold would be maintained. Internal trade on the other hand would be promoted by a new independent state institution, which, by system of book entries, would purchase the whole production of certain specified industries and issue corresponding means of exchange. The state would not, of course, take over any goods which individual concerns saw fit to produce. Questionnaires would first be circulated among producers and consumers and thus fairly accurate data obtained in advance regarding potential production and the needs and wants of customers. On the basis of this information the quantities of the different goods which the State could buy would be calculated and the figures published, thus affording producers the stimulus of a certain guaranteed sale.

Mr. Medbøe maintains that an enormous increase in prosperity would result if internal production and distribution were made independent of gold and the international situation and fostered in the way he specifies.

The position of the Norwegian Krone abroad would be made more secure than at present, since the Norwegian Bank could devote its gold reserves to, and concentrate exclusively on, the country's foreign trade.

The new state institution would fix suitable conditions and prices for internal trade. Exporting industries would naturally have to adjust themselves to the conditions imposed by foreign competition but Mr. Medbøe thinks that the internal institution which would gain control of such great resources that exports could without difficulty be subsidized therefrom if need be and wages and salaries maintained at a uniform level in all industries.

Coming from a banker and a man of Mr. Medbøe's varied administrative experience the plan merits especial interest.

The barrister and economist, Hans J. Utne, well known in Norway for his broadcast talks on economic subjects, has advanced an extremely lucid plan for a credit guarantee fund based on rational principles of insurance. Whereas Mr. Medbøe would divorce internal from foreign trade Mr. Utne would make a distinction between the monetary system and the credit system.

According to Mr. Utne the function of a monetary system, which is essentially of a static nature, is to keep the value of money relatively stable, whereas the essentially dynamic function of the credit system is to regulate those circumstances which decide economic development and to exploit protective possibilities. "The center of gravity of all trade has today moved from the monetary to the credit system," writes Mr. Utne, "and the latter cannot simply be guided by principles which regulate the former and vice versa. When the monetary system is made to embrace both functions the result is that either the one or the other is neglected. During the war the question of the stability of money was temporarily shelved and unlimited credit was allowed. After the war the credit system was sacrificed in order that the monetary system might be stabilized. This was jumping out of the frying pan into the fire!"

Mr. Utne then quotes instances of fluctuations in the volume of credit which have meant ruin and starvation for thousands and he shows that they are often completely independent of the volume of money in the narrower sense, and of the price level. There have been cases where, though the volume of money has remained constant, or even increased, the volume of credit has fallen by as much as 50% without the occurrence of any natural catastrophe or any exceptional rise in production during the period in question.

Thereupon Mr. Utne advances to schemes, which would be complementary to, but also independent of, each other. The first consists in the separation of the credit system from the money system and the institution of the Credit Center, either as an independent organization or as a department of the Norwegian Bank. Since it is the credit system which actually controls the productive life of the country this suggestion bears a certain resemblance to Medbøe's plan.

If such a Credit Center were set up and competently administered so that it could be ascertained when, where and how much Credit should be issued, whence would it derive the power to execute its plans? Utne's other proposal for a Credit Guarantee Fund enters in here. All who benefit by credit must also be prepared to share the risks involved. It is insecurity which prevents a sufficient issue of credit today and in the absence of such credit it has been vain to hope for a return of that "private initiative" and "confidence" which are dependent on a normal flow of credit! As the primary beneficiaries and interested parties would, as in insurance, contribute to the Credit Guarantee Fund premiums, the aggregate of which would cover the greater part of all risks involved. The balance would be borne by the community as a whole, which also to an extent enjoys benefits deriving from a free flow of credit. This slight burden would be more than offset by the advantages accruing to such a scientific credit administration.

An extremely able work of its kind is Professor Keilhau's *Overgang til ny Pengeenhet (Transition to a New Unit of Currency)* in which he traces the history of those monetary measures which are behind Dr. Eisler's proposal and, moreover, gives a heap of valuable information regarding monetary conditions up till the present day. Most applicable to our problems is his chapter on *The Central Bank and the State,* in which he writes as follows: "The recognition of the constitutional character of the monetary system... was expressed from the middle ages onwards in the contention that the issue of money, which at that time meant minted coins, must be a royal prerogative.

"...However, it was not at once recognized in all countries that banknotes have the same function as coinage and that, therefore, the issue of banknotes should be made subject to the approval of, and conditions imposed by, the state...In the 20th century, however, the view has everywhere come to be adopted that the state as the sovereign authority has the right to forbid private persons to issue banknotes and consequently also has the right to allow one or more private institutions to issue this form of currency on conditions fixed by the proper authorities of the state."

Drawn to its logical conclusion Professor Keilhau's argument would imply that, just as it was eventually recognized that banknotes have the same function as coins, so it should now be recognized that credit means of exchange have the same function as both coinage and bank notes. Above all it must be borne in mind that credit means of exchange now form by far the greater part of all means of exchange, or of "money" in the popular sense. Hence if the state control of the monetary system is still thought desirable it must follow that the state should have the same control of credit. It has, of course, already a certain authority in the matter but not to that extent whereby an expedient issue of credit, corresponding to the community's needs and potential productiveness, is assured. Thus we are led back to the central theme in the proposals of Douglas, Soddy, and Eisler, namely, an issue of credit in proportion to real productive powers.

CHAPTER 10

COMPARISONS

A ll schemes of reform have two aspects: firstly they involve a certain control of the *volume* of the means of distribution, in order that this volume may come definitely related to the volume of goods and services. Secondly the reforms are intended to influence the *circulation* of the means of distribution—this applies both to the speed (and for some proposals) to the *direction* of the circulation.

The schemes described in this book are all based on the realization of the great physical wealth of the modern world, which exists side by side with a huge potential but ineffective demand, and also on the vital need of reforming our obsolete economic mechanism.

The methods of reform are of two kinds. Firstly, there are those which involve merely the planning and control of the means of distribution, in order that these may become definitely related to the goods and services which exist, and secondly, there are those which would not only plan and control the means of distribution, but would allocate them in a certain way.

Many supporters of "stabilized money" consider that things will automatically adjust themselves when the retail price-level is kept constant. Where stabilized money has been introduced, however, as; for example, in Sweden, although it has shown itself to have many advantages, it has not radically improved trade nor essentially decreased unemployment or poverty, the reason being that the issue of credit has not been affected.

Although one experiment does not necessarily prove

the method to be inadequate, it is considered so by the many economists who pointed out its limitations long before this practical experiment was carried out. Among those who have most successfully shown the independence of the stability of money from the volume of credit is the Norwegian economist and lawyer, Hans J. Utne. He points to the increase in the volume of credit in the USA between 1925 and 1933, and especially between 1925 and 1929. Fluctuations in the price-level were never more than 5% during that period so that the value of money was fairly stable, though on the whole the price-level sank, and the number of bank notes in circulation decreased slightly. Thus there seemed to be a slight deflation.

During the same period credit activity was as follows. Loans to stockbrokers rose between 1925 and 1929 from 3 to 5 millard dollars, i.e. by 65%. The issue of credit to industry during the same period increased by 12%. The rate of interest of "Call Loans" rose from 4 to 7.6%. But in spite of the decrease in the amount of currency, the fall in prices and the doubling of the rate of interest, there was nevertheless a definite increase in the volume of credit, which followed its own course.

Prominent supporters of stabilized money are fully aware of this fact. Men like Irving Fisher, J. M. Keynes and many others point out that before stabilizing the value of money, credit must be controlled. Roosevelt's politics are an obvious result of this point of view, as are those of the United Kingdom and countries on sterling after the "Imperial Declaration". Eisler has also suggested that credit should be deliberately increased to correspond to the productive possibilities which now exist.

In his plans for the future, Professor Fisher contributes a noteworthy addition to the economic literature of the last few years. These plans, given an outline in *Stabilized Money*, involve the central control of the credit system, the relating of credit to actual productive power, and the direct issue by the community of interest-free stock to cover interest-bearing debt, "checking accounts backed by 100% lawful money".

Characteristically enough, Professor Fisher covers over two pages of his most recent book in the appreciation and quotation of Soddy. He also pays a tribute to Douglas on account of his persistent demonstration of the objections to a fluctuating value of money. Apart from this, he does not touch on the Social Credit proposals.

Professor Soddy, on the other hand, has precisely defined the similarities and differences between his point of view and that of Social Credit. He considers that under Social Credit the annual issue of the National Dividend would bring money onto the market which would not circulate. Only at the moment when goods are actually available does Soddy propose to increase the volume of credit. This would be used either for new production or for repayment of debt. He agrees with issuing part of his credit directly to the consumer, but then only once and for all, and cannot until there is an actual increase in available goods. In a private letter to the author (29 July, 1933) he writes: "On the rack and pinion analogy, with the rack for the monetary situation and the pinion for the unending distribution of goods from production to consumption (an endless quantity of goods for *one* finite quantity of money) we both agree that the pinion must be increased to send forward a much larger volume of goods. But where I do it once and for all (to arrive at a given maximum rate of production), in Major Douglas's scheme, as I understand it, the pinion is increased (new money is issued) *every time it goes round.*"

If the National Dividend were distributed each year as a fixed sum, which corresponded to the eventual maximum productive power of the community, Soddy's criticism would certainly be valid. But since it is merely a small annual issue the object of which is gradually to increase production to its full capacity, there is no other difference between Soddy's and Douglas's procedure in this respect than that the one seeks accurately to follow the increasing production, and the other, to issue vast amounts in even installments year-by-year. As I have previously pointed out, the National Dividend is not new money, since it finds its way back to its source in the National

Credit Office and is increased in volume only when there is an increase in production.

Soddy questions Douglas's assertion that at present there is always too little purchasing power, that the aggregate price of all goods is more than that of wages and earnings. Douglas and his supporters have replied by pointing to the accounts of various interdependent industries. But since Soddy is also in agreement with a direct issue of purchasing power, there cannot be a very wide divergence of opinion on this point.

The real difference between Soddy and Douglas is that the latter would finance new production with new credit, whereas the former would do so with savings. Abstention from consumption is necessary, he says, before we can produce. Not until goods are actually in existence should the necessary due credit be issued. The difference between them, therefore, lies chiefly in the time factor. One mortgages future energy, while the other builds on earlier saving.

Soddy recognizes the truth of the analysis of the Technocrats, who have been greatly influenced by him, but he considers the scheme of energy certificates to be too little developed and too undefined even to warrant discussion.

The Technocrats realize that their analysis of the present system is similar to that of all the New Economists, but they accuse these of only going halfway. There can be no compromise they say, with the system in which the standard of measurement is this variable as a concertina. They maintained that in an age of kilowatts, the means of distribution should also be expressed in units of energy.

Mr. Orage, the late editor of the *New English Weekly*, has written a characteristic answer to this. He has written that (the Technocrat) B. Jones's principle of "mortgaging the future" is very similar to Social Credit. Since debt must equal the cost of production, the money system makes it impossible for the producer to receive all costs of production from the consumer. Even if President Roosevelt uses free state credit for reflation and for his work schemes, he will have to turn to new brains if

America is to make use of its own wealth. The Technocrats' positive contribution will thus depend on their ability to find a money system, based not on energy but quite simply on purchasing power. Rationing and dictatorship would be rendered unnecessary by a credit system which accurately reflected the industrial system. The transfer of goods from the producer to the consumer cannot be accomplished by the calculation of the horsepower required to produce the goods but quite simply by that of the cost of producing and selling them.

Mr. Orage's point of view, like that of Professor Soddy, is perhaps somewhat biased. Technically there should be no difficulty in introducing energy certificates, and even if the matter has not been worked out in detail, the main idea is clear enough. It would however be a revolutionary reform especially from a psychological point of view. Both Social Credit and Soddy's plan allow easier and more simple solutions, since they would adapt the existing system, using the same kind of money and the same framework.

Free Economy has had a little recognition outside Germany, Austria and Switzerland, with the exception of Professor Fisher's experiment with the "stamp dollar" in some parts of America. Through this experiment the Free Economists have undoubtedly influenced the Technocrats, though this is not generally admitted.

Professor Fisher writes appreciatively of the Free Economists and Silvio Gesell in *Booms and Depressions* (1933) and also in *Stabilized Money* (1935) in which he says: "He seems to be the first to consider the problem of controlling the velocity of circulation for the purpose of influencing the value of money." He adds, however, that "the only part of Gesell's program which I have endorsed is his stamped currency proposal—and that without accepting his belief that it would lead to the abolition of interest."

Free Economy would control only the distributive mechanism but Soddy and Douglas maintain that not only should the credit system be state-controlled, but also to a certain extent, the productive system. Apart from this, there is a similarity between Free Economy and Social Credit in their respective proposals of depreciating currency and consumer credit. Both methods would accelerate distribution. Social Credit's purchasing premium, however, which would depend on industrial industrial expansion, has not the disadvantages to the consumer of depreciating currency. It is also more elastic and adaptable.

Eisler, too, proposes to relate money and credit to potential production but without any further interference with the existing system than international agreement and the proportional issues of credit necessitate.

The scheme which has lately been most discussed and criticized is Social Credit, chiefly on account of the intense propaganda of which the movement supporting it has carried out in England, the Dominions and in other countries. The matter has also been debated in public, notably between Douglas and Professor D. H. Robertson on the wireless in 1933, between Douglas and R.G. Hawtry (Director of Financial Studies in the British Treasury) in Birmingham in 1933, and in the Marshall Society of Cambridge in October 1934. A number of excellent books on the scheme have also been published and the Social Credit press promptly answers all its critics.

I will now deal with the chapter called *Four Monetary Heretics* by H. T. N. Gaitskell from G. D. H. Cole's book, *What Everybody Wants to Know about Money,* (Victor Gollancz, 1933). The four heretics are Gesell, Soddy, Douglas and Eisler. The chapter is therefore of particular interest to us here.

Mr. Gaitskell's criticisms appear to be sincere but are insufficiently well-informed. He deals with Silvio Gesell with great thoroughness and a certain amount of appreciation. He thinks that depreciation currency would not necessarily prevent either usury or saving, for instance in the case when prices fall quicker than the money depreciates. Like the Norwegian economist, Thorolf Winter-Hjelm, he comes to the conclusion that Free Economy would not prevent economic depressions, since these are due not only to saving and variations in the velocity of circulation, which are, however, without doubt important causes. Free Economy, he thinks, is likely to bring only temporary alleviation, as the experiments in Bavaria and Austria have shown.

Gaitskell gives an account of the experiment in Wörgl in Austria, in which "tickets for services rendered" were issued as money, which depreciated in value with time.

Mr. Gaitskell's university colleague, Professor Frederick Soddy, is accorded nine patronizing pages. "Professor Frederick Soddy, M.A., F.R.S., is, as the letters after his name imply, a very distinguished man," he says. In these nine pages he explains Soddy's proposals and his own objections to them in an elegant and witty manner. He writes: "These fictitious loans may be wicked, but are they also the cause of industrial depression? Professor Soddy evidently believes that they are, but his reasons for this belief are not always very clear." Gaitskell's principal objection to Soddy is that he mixes economics with morals. If by this he means that economics are unconnected with morality he is obviously wrong. All economic legislation and procedure today have a moral basis, though possibly an obsolete and objectionable one. It is just as much a crime against the existing moral law of "he that does not work, neither shall he eat" to house and feed the poor without any exchange of work, as it is to make money on financial transactions without any corresponding efforts. Whether or not this morality is sound is another matter. Douglas strongly denies it.

If Mr. Gaitskell means that economics and morality are unconnected he is talking nonsense, but if he means that those particular moral principles which Soddy advances are wrong, he should have made this clear. Soddy has replied to Gaitskell in an article in *New Britain*.

Gaitskell, however, recognizes his colleague's valuable study of fictitious loans and their effects, which he began in 1924, before any other economist had taken up the matter. But in spite of this original contribution, Gaitskell considers that Soddy's enthusiasm and moral indignation have brought him to too hasty conclusions; "any stick is good enough" is a motto suitable to the real zealot. Gaitskell also recognizes that Soddy supported the stabilization of prices before this was a general tendency.

He adds that there is no doubt of the importance of the questions which Soddy considers, but his treatment of him, he thinks, is specious. He concludes by saying: "Soddy would have served better his own purpose of acquiring the knowledge of 'how to secure the fruits of what we already possess', had he exercised in his economic studies the same detached perseverance as must have been displayed in his work in natural science." There is however, in the whole of this essay no indication that Gaitskell has grasped the essentials of Professor Soddy's work as expressed in his *An Energy Theory of Wealth*, undoubtedly a point of view which Mr. Gaitskell should consider.

Gaitskell devotes the greatest amount space to Douglas —as many as 29 pages, which includes several diagrams. Unfortunately it is the weakest and least scientific of the four sections. It is the more regrettable in that a refutation in this case would have been of the greatest interest since the scheme is the one with the widest support.

Gaitskell uses a considerable part of his valuable space in disproving what are actually misinterpretations of the Douglas plan. He claims that Douglas is ambiguous and can be understood in several ways, and he cheerfully proceeds to disprove a number of theories which are not those of Douglas at all, though he afterwards admits that perhaps he has misunderstood his meaning. But it is curious that in writing scientific work of this kind he should not have made certain exactly what Douglas does mean, if by no other method than that of personal contact either with Douglas himself, who lives in the same town, or with one of those economists who support him. It is equally curious that he should not have been able to obtain a clear understanding from such a book as *The Monopoly of Credit*. Apparently he has read neither this work nor Douglas's latest –*Social Credit*. He quotes only from books 10 years old and from pamphlets which Douglas himself has not written. From these he convinces himself that Douglas is ambiguous.

Admitted that Douglas's style is challenging, but his meaning is clear. For our part, the whole of his collected works have cost us less effort to understand than these 29 pages of Gaitskell.

Twenty two of the twenty nine pages are devoted to the so-called "A plus B" theory. Now, this theory is not the most simple of Douglas's conclusions. He seeks thereby to demonstrate why there is at present always too little purchasing power compared with prices. He calls all payments to individuals, that is all purchasing power, A payments, and all others, those for raw materials, plant depreciation charges, etc. he calls B payments. He says that A alone can never be sufficient to cover A plus B. A more thorough explanation than this is needed, however, to make the matter clear, of what is meant by A and B, how the time factor enters in and so on. But this theory does not affect the main point of Social Credit, which is the relating of credits to actual productive power and the state control of the credit system and hence indirectly of production.

Expressed shortly in pamphlet form this A plus B theory is likely to give rise to many different interpretations, but in *The Monopoly of Credit* (1931) Douglas has precisely explained it.

Having delved laboriously through obsolete books and anonymous brochures, Gaitskell comes to the conclusion that there are five possible interpretations of the theory; (we could have supplied him with many more.) Gaitskell then admits that purchasing power is less than the aggregate of prices, but that the gap between them is considerably less than Douglas thinks, and he maintains that this gap is caused only by the writing off of capital, but is lessened however, by the simultaneous paying out of wages in the manufacture of new plant. By this Gaitskell means that these payments are less than the aggregate writing off of capital, so that ultimately there is always a small gap.

Whether Douglas, the price expert, or Gaitskell, the lecturer on economics, is the better judge of the size of this gap, or whether there is any permanent gap at all, is of less interest than the patent insufficiency purchasing power the whole world over.

Social Credit is sufficiently real to be independent of mere theoretical argument, and in the remaining seven pages of his criticism Gaitskell gives an interesting account of the proposals.

In dealing with the Just Price, he maintains that even if the gap between prices and purchasing power did not exist, this procedure would not necessarily have an inflationary effect. Those who claim that it would, do Douglas an injustice, he says, since the producer would of course be credited only on condition that there was a fall in prices. On the other hand, he considers that this measure would not in the long run be of any use, since the same difficulty would be met with as exists today, i.e. the inability of the banks to renew loans and overdrafts. In the same way, the state would not be able to renew its credit, if there were no permanent fall in prices.

Apart from this, he thinks that the technical difficulties of such price control would be enormous. He apparently forgets Douglas's final suggestion of issuing credit direct to the consumer, keeping prices as they are.

In dealing with the extent of the deficit in purchasing power, Gaitskell remarks that the calculations which Major Douglas and his followers have made are both curious and surprising, and quite inaccurate. Douglas, however, has never attempted to define the size of the deficit. He has given examples for particular cases, but he has never mentioned that it is possible to obtain an exact average figure, nor that it is necessary to do so. The price reduction which he suggests– about 25%–is merely a beginning and is not intended to immediately cancel out the total gap. Thus, when Gaitskell remarks that the size of the price reduction does not appear to have any connection with his analysis in his earlier works, he merely reveals that he has not made a proper study of them. Douglas has certainly developed his ideas during the last 10 years, as he has a perfect right to do, but the development is a natural one and does not turn from one extreme to the other, as in the case of many other economic writers.

Gaitskell ends by saying: "It is not for his conviction but also for his methods that Major Douglas must be regarded as a religious rather than a scientific reformer." If he means by this that Douglas deals with other sides of the social life than the strictly economic (which actually cannot be isolated from them) he is quite right. But if he means that there is an insufficiently scientific basis to Douglas's arguments, he is recommended to compare his own contribution with Douglas's *The Monopoly of Credit*. Anyone making a thorough study of Douglas's writings will discover that he most certainly does not bring in any irrelevant morality or sentimentality, but on the contrary pitilessly exposes the sentimentality and illogicality of the present system.

Gaitskell accords Eisler eleven pages. He begins by praising him for his knowledge of economic history and for his understanding of the last crisis, and he infers that it may perhaps appear strange that he should have included a man of such worth among the heretics.

If Mr. Gaitskell had studied Eisler with that seriousness which he is apparently entitled to, he would have spared himself a lot of trouble. In his criticism of Eissler he is guilty of a blatant mistake in the very beginning. On this he builds up his whole criticism which therefore has no validity.

Gaitskell postulates that during a certain period of time credit increases in volume by $1/10$. He says that if the whole of this new credit is changed into current money and exchange for retail commodities, according to Dr. Eisler, we should anticipate a rise in prices of $1/10$, since if the retailer does not increase his gross receipts by $1/10$, if receipts after the alteration in the rate of exchange between current and bank money has been announced.

Now, Eisler has tried to show in his *Stable Money*, by statistics and diagrams, that prices never rise proportionately with the issue of credit at the beginning of the period of expansion, but at a much slower rate. Only much later on do prices begin to rise at the same rate. On this fact rests the whole of Eisler's argument.

It is remarkable that Gaitskell, who poses as the critic of critics, should not have understood this and should give a wrong explanation of the "quantity theory" that prices are in inverse proportion to the amount of money and credit. He even states that "according to Dr. Eisler" this is so!

He writes: "We may presume therefore that he (Eisler) will rely for his stimulus on the rise in wholesale prices. This may of course come about in a perfectly straightforward way from the increased bank credit. Now Dr. Eisler thinks that this will take place at the expense only of the potential buyer of wholesale goods. But he is forgetting the retailer. What is his position? He takes exactly the same gross receipts expressed in terms of bank money; his *other* expenses–rent and wages– remain unchanged in terms of bank money, but the cost of his stock increases in direct proportion to the rise in wholesale prices. The profitability of his concerns therefore must steadily decline–the increased output of wholesale goods will remain unsold and their prices will fall again." The whole of his argument is based on this false premise.

Finally Gaitskell comes to the "graver objection that, in laying stress on the increase in consumers' incomes in the later stages of the boom, Dr. Eisler is fundamentally wrong. For, as we have seen, it is in the investment goods trades that the depression first sets it. If on the other hand the maintenance of consumers' incomes were secured in the early stages of a boom, the expansion of the investment goods trades might be checked..."

Eisler has nowhere suggested that his scheme should be put into operation during the later stages of a boom. Those proposals of his which were advanced at the World Economic Conference were planned to be put into operation immediately, either to induce or accelerate the boom which was expected after the long depression, and to last throughout and after the boom period. That crises begin in the heavy industries is what Eisler points out again and again. His whole scheme is conditioned by this fact.

On top of these blunders, Gaitskell somewhat logically concludes that: "While therefore we cannot accept Dr. Eisler's analysis, there are certain features of his positive proposals which might, in a rather different way, prove valuable."

After dealing with the four heretics, Gaitskell writes a conclusion. He complains therein principally of their obscurity and maintains that this is the reason both for their popularity and for the extreme difficulty in criticizing them. He says: "To the plain man and the heretic alike the natural limitation to material welfare is essentially technical. That quite apart from this, there should be almost as inevitable and difficult a problem of the organization, of relations, is a vision confined as a rule to the expert who has to handle it." But, who, may we ask, is this expert? Is he Mr. Gaitskell himself, or Vincent Vickers, a director of the Bank of England for nine years and a supporter of Eisler's proposals, or Eisler himself, the renowned monetary historian, or Douglas, the price expert? Where is your clarity of thought here, Mr. Gaitskell?

"Every monetary heretic offers a single complete solution. The *one* thing alone has to be done. A unique masterstroke is required– the one perfectly simple, perfectly feasible PLAN." Here is another lamentable proof of Gaitskell's ignorance of his subjects. Not one of the heretics with whom he deals is of the opinion that "one perfectly simple, perfectly feasible technical alteration" will put everything right. Each one of them, especially Soddy and Douglas, has pointed out that a thorough reorganization in every direction is needed, and that its execution may take decades or even centuries to accomplish, the situation in the world today being as it is. To point out existing possibilities is nonetheless profitable for that.

Following on this Mr. Gaitskell's well meant concluding

words are not very convincing. He writes: "These comments are not intended to imply any criticism of heretical writing. On the contrary it is of the utmost importance that every individual should be free to express himself on economic affairs. The plain man's instinct is in this case right. Economic experts can never be wholly trusted, and only with the utmost possible freedom for criticism and construction can rapid scientific progress being made."

One of the latest attacks on Social Credit comes in a book by W. R. Hiskett, which has a foreword by Dr. Hugh Dalton. The title of the book puts before the reader the strange alternative of *Social Credit or Socialism* (Gollancz, Ltd. 1935). Having read it, I wondered whether the whole thing was a joke or possibly a piece of camouflage propaganda for the Douglas scheme, but I have been assured on good authority that the work is actually meant to be a serious criticism of the proposals. The Social Credit movement can best be congratulated on a piece of free and very effective propaganda. No doubt the book will soon be replied to and refuted by the movement. Here I will deal with only two of the points involved.

Mr. Hiskett is perfectly right in claiming that to subsidize the consumer would result in inflation, but only so long as the existing forms of credit issue, loans, interest, etc. are retained. Mr. Hiskett like so many other critics has not sufficiently realized –has not perhaps been sufficiently conscientious in examining–the nature and scope of the Douglas proposals, particularly in the matter of the issue of purchasing power.

He is also right in stating that every beginner in the study of economics knows that credit expansion results in inflation and a rise in prices, for it is *only* the beginner who believes this today. Facts show that the matter is not so simple. For example between 1925 and 1929 in the USA there was a fall in wholesale prices of 3 to 5% but loans to stockbrokers rose by 65% and loans to industry by 12%. In Sweden during the last four years the retail price level has never varied more than 2%, in spite of the Kreuger crash, the financing of large public works and big fluctuations in the foreign exchange. A rise of prices during installation is therefore not inevitable. The matter is complicated and requires a thorough consideration in each individual case.

Another common misunderstanding is that concerning the *right ownership*, a much abused phrase. In what meaning can it be applied to the debt-burdened industrialist of today? No doubt he would be able more truthfully to call himself an owner under Social Credit than at present, but even then with considerable limitations imposed by the interests of the community. This matter of ownership is not a simple one. It does not mean the same thing today as it did in the Stone Age, and the notion that the private ownership of the means of production prevents the consumer from obtaining his rightful share displays only ignorance of the function of money.

Most economists even among those who are well disposed towards Social Credit are inclined to misunderstand the A plus B theory. In a short form it can be explained most adequately in the following manner, which has been taken from Mr. A. W. Joseph's mathematical exposition in the *New Age* of the 8th of November, 1934: In order that sufficient purchasing power may be issued to buy the products of industry, more and more it must be spent on capital development. The result is an unbalanced tendency towards the manufacture of further means of production at the expense of consumable goods. This epitomizes the A plus B theorem, and suggests a very good reason why, as all economists are aware, every improvement begins in the industries producing capital goods.

The opposition between the so-called heretical and orthodox points of view on this and similar matters seems likely to give way to a mutual understanding. Professor Fisher's proposals, for instance, which he expresses in *Stabilized Money* are among the most promising of recent times. These and similar results are without doubt due to the intense efforts in propaganda of the reform movements discussed here. Their critics have also played a part in bringing these vitally important problems before the notice of the general public, with a result that they are beginning to have a marked effect in the political field.

CHAPTER 11

CONCLUSION

The Norwegian industrialist, Mr. S. Kloutmann, who has held responsible positions in a number of different industries and is now managing director of the Norwegian Aluminum Company, in an address to the Norwegian Association of Civil Engineers, January 1935, spoke as follows:

"Our progress has been such that we today live in a world where productive power in practically all spheres of industry is many times greater, or perhaps I should say, in order to avoid any possible fear of contradiction, 100% greater than is our consuming power. In other words, our productive resources are far in excess of our distributive resources. We are fettered by obsolete conceptions inherited from the time when the world was not capable satisfying all human needs. The colossal contributions of technique to industry have essentially altered the nature of the world's problems. This indubitable fact is either not understood or else not admitted by a great many people. During these times of depression we have lived surrounded by abundance; our great fault has been a refusal to undertake that reorganization which our plenty so obviously demands. We have sought to remain within the bounds of the old system which was planned for a world in the process of construction, suffering from a scarcity of goods.

"The fact is that our material development has been so rapid that few have been able intellectually or socially to adapt themselves accordingly. Few have been able to recognize that the "saturation point" has been reached and that we must change our whole mentality. Many men, some of great influence in the affairs of the world, recognize this, and it is therefore to be hoped that we are on the way to a happier order of society.

"The one great problem today is how, in a practical way, which gives full rein to the force of individual initiative, to distribute among all countries and all peoples the endless bounty of the world."

All who have some knowledge of our immense untapped technical resources will agree that Mr. Kloumann has been restrained in his estimate. And in this he is wise, for every day fresh discoveries are made and new processes evolved, so that nobody can have a clear conception of our enormous possibilities. On the day that conditions permit a full use of the apparatus of production, the results will utterly stupefy the uninitiated.

The extent of our underconsumption at the moment is preposterous. Masses of men, women and children are being permanently stunted, physically and mentally, through undernourishment.

Neither is there any lack of manpower or of will to work. About 25 million souls in the world are officially registered as seeking employment and these probably represent only a fraction of the unused labor available. The managing director of one of Norway's largest industrial concerns, speaking at the general meeting of his company in March 1935 said: "One of the most tragic things I know are the daily applications for work which we receive; yet we are already overstaffed." This is a typical state of affairs.

It is unprofitable to impute claim to this or that section of the community but we are at all points forced to admit the inadequacy of our present system of distribution. I think that probably in the not very distant future we shall have no choice but to revolutionize that system on the lines indicated by the New Economists, that is to say by raising purchasing power to productivity.

What are the implications of the New Economics, and what does the future hold in store? Its most obvious implications are of course greater freedom and leisure for the individual, and a release from Adam's curse, the necessity for toil.

A common objection to the exploitation of the great productive powers of the world is the moral one that people would lose their healthy respect for work. But does the present situation with its growing unemployment and taxation encourage or facilitate this respect? Moreover everyone surely has a right to his share of the cultural heritage which our forefathers have handed down to us, and which would afford economic independence and freedom to every individual, thus allowing him to choose his own vocation and to pay for his own education. It is surely an underestimation of human nature to consider that people would lose respect for work merely because they had a few pounds in their pockets? Actual fact proves it to be so.

To have economic independence is on the contrary likely to bring out the best in the individual, by enabling him to choose his own occupation and follow his own bent. That so many people are thwarted in this respect today is one of the chief reasons for the present discontent and revolt in the world. It should be possible today to allow everyone to be his own master, rather than, as he usually is, as slaves under an obsolete financial system.

In *Economic Democracy*, Douglas writes: "In respect of any undertaking, centralization is the way to do it, but is not the correct method of deciding what to do or of selecting the individual who is to do it."

In the same work, he writes also: "Systems were made for man, and not men for systems, and the interest of men which is self development, is above all systems, whether theological, political or economic."

Given economic independence, it is unreasonable to suppose that people would not take to some respectable occupation, though it is possible that few would choose manual work. No more is now necessary, however, than would afford a little healthy exercise and be willingly performed.

It is obvious that the more the machine displaces human labor the less obligations there should be for the individual to expend his energies in purely economic directions, and the more leisure and freedom he should possess. There should today be no moral stigma attached even to complete inactivity and "lotus-eating" if this is the somewhat unlikely desire of the individual.

Man is creative and will always find an outlet for his energies when these are not entirely absorbed by economic necessity—in sport, art or science for instance. That we would die of boredom or take to crime if we were to toil for no more than a few hours a week to obtain food, warmth and shelter (which is likely soon to be all that is necessary) is the strange and blind conception which the struggle for existence has given us.

Let us take the case of art. How many people alive today forced by economic necessity to do work they do not enjoy, desire more than anything the leisure and freedom in which to express their true selves. Today the artist is usually forced either to abandon his profession, to prostitute it or to starve. Genius will always be recognized in the end, and hardship stimulates it, declare those who are afraid of change, but athough mental and spiritual adversity may be stimulants, an empty stomach leads but to the grave. A sane economic system would give full scope to artistic creation.

Another field for activity is that of sport and the cult of the body. There is also the cult of the mind, an equally ancient, if today not so highly respected, pastime. In this sphere, therapeutic psychology has within recent years made considerable advances, and is becoming of increasing importance, in a world growing ever more neurotic under the economic stress. In the Leisure Age it is likely to become not merely analytic but also synthetic, and to be of use in discovering the hidden talents in each individual and in leading him in the right direction from birth onwards to the attainment of a full, creative and satisfying life. It is likely also to be able to master the hitherto unconquerable impulses of man, and to displace punishment in the treatment of crime.

Today even religion is warped by economic circumstances, and, instead of freeing mankind, binds him even tighter to a false morality. Once the economic pressure is released its true interpretation as a profound relaxation of the self will surely revive.

In every walk of human life, we should now be on the road to developments which we can only begin to foresee, if only this one difficulty of *money* were solved. It is often supposed that before this problem can be solved, the political confusion must first be clarified. This, however, is the result of the defective monetary system, and is therefore subsidiary to it. A truer realization of the existing economic possibilities would automatically alter the political outlook, not towards complete unity, for that is a Utopian ideal, and not even desirable, but towards a more pertinent and less bitter struggle.

If chaos is to give place to a rational social economic system, the first requisite is that the general public shall realize the present vast productive powers of the world, which has been hinted at in this review. The decision ultimately rests with the mass of the people, once they have grasped the issue at stake. Is it to be restriction or development, destruction or distribution?

Translators' Appendix

In support of Mr. Björset's concluding paragraph, we append the following facts and figures without comment. We are indebted for the majority of them to Mr. Palme Dutt's *Fascism and Social Revolution*, Mr. Maurice Colbourne's *Economic Nationalism*, Mr. John Hodgson's *The Great God Waste*, and to the Green Shirts' *Attack*.

I

MACHINE-MADE WEALTH

In Hausleiter's *Revolution in der Weltwirtschaft* (1932) the growth of industrial machine power in the world in millions of horsepower is given as follows (one horse power is commonly calculated as equivalent to the muscular power of six men):

1835 ...	... 0.65
1875 ...	... 26.5
1913 ...	... 211
1928 ...	... 390

"In the century since 1835, industrial machine power multiplied 100 times in England, and 600 times in the whole world–and has ended in mass starvation and unemployment without equal." (Palme Dutt). Stewart Chase in his *Machines and Men* (1929) has estimated that the machine power of the world as representing the muscular power of 9000 million additional men, or a equivalent to five slaves for every man, woman and child of the human race.

Between the first and second World Power Conferences in 1924 and 1930, electrical output doubled from 150,000 million units to 300,000 million units. (*Economist,* 21st June, 1930).

Between 1890 and 1921, according to the report of the senior trade commissioner in Canada for May 1930, further mechanization of agriculture and extension of the area of cultivation have multiplied the yield of wheat per agricultural worker fivefold; and as the most revolutionary machine, the combined reaper and thresher, was only introduced in 1924, the output per worker must now be a great deal higher.

Between 1900 and the 1924-8 the harvests of all cereals increased in Australia 104%, in the Argentine 172%, and in Canada 300%. Between 1913 and 1928 the volume of world grain exports increased 147%. In the same period world population increased 11.6%.

World stocks of primary products, on the basis of 1923-5 as 100, increased by the end of 1926 to 134, by 1928 to 161, by 1929 to 192, by 1930 to 235, by 1931 to 263, and by the end of 1932, despite all the destruction of stocks, still stood at 263, or more than two and a half times the volume of eight years before. (*Economist,* May 6th, 1933)

"The United States Commissioner for Labor Statistics recently stated that if 200 out of the 1357 boot and shoe factories in the country works full-time, they could satisfy the whole existing demand, and the remaining 1157 establishments could be closed down. Similarly, 1487 out of the 6057 bituminous coal mines could produce all the coal that was needed." (H.B. Butler in the *International Labor Review,* March 1931.)

"The statement has been made many times that American factories in the main industries could more than supply the world's needs, even if all other supply sources closed down." (H.C. Armitage in a paper to the *Institute of Automobile Engineers.*)

In 1879, 41,695 men produced 3,070,875 tons of pig iron in the USA. In 1929, 24,960 men produced 42,613,983 tons of pig iron in the USA.

From these figures it can be calculated that in 50 years the productivity of pig iron has increased 23.2 times.

The turbine type of engine came in about 1900. We now have turbine units of 300,000 hp: 3 million times the work capacity of a man on an eight hour basis, or 9 million times on a twenty-four 24 hour basis.

Professor Frederick Soddy estimates that the productive capacity of Great Britain has increased, since the introduction of mechanical power, some 4000%.

In 1933 the famous Bata boot factory at Zlinn, in Czechoslovakia, reported the invention of a machine which needed only to be fed with leather and thread. Then, without any human agency, it proceeds to manufacture boots and shoes, which need only the insertion of laces to be ready for wear. (The machine is not being used, not because it is inefficient, but because it is too efficient, and would, if operated, throw too many people out of work.)

A lamp making machine, also invented in 1933, would enable the German Osram Company to supply the whole requirements of the German market in a few weeks if the new machine were allowed to operate continuously at full capacity.

The following figures given by the president of the US Chamber of Commerce as long ago as 1926, are typical of industry as a whole:

One man, with one bottle-making machine, replaces 54 men.

One girl, with six rib-cutting machines, replaces 25 girls.

Two men, with one coal conveyor, replace 50 men.

One man, with one cigarette-wrapping machine, replaces 100 men.

League of Nations figures quoted by the Macmillan Report show that while the world's population increased 10% between 1913 and 1928, its production of food during that period increased 16%.

The discovery of how to make nitrates synthetically reduced Chile's export of natural nitrates from 2,000,000 tons in 1923 to one and a third million tons in 1925. At present, therefore, the world is overstocked with a food forcing chemical.

Professor Soddy estimated that 4000 men equipped with modern machinery could produce the whole of the USA wheat crop.

A single Californian hatchery, with an incubator capacity of 500,000 eggs at a time, hatches 3 million chickens a year by electricity. Again, 4 to 6 cows can be milked at one time with an electric milker , of which in 1926 there were some 100,000 in the USA alone.

1933, according to the *Sunday Express,* was installed in the city office of one of the big five banks, a machine 4 feet high. Operated by one girl and doing the work of 60 bank clerks, this machine deals with 60,000 separate ledger entries in an hour; it records the code numbers of the client and the check, the amounts paid in or out, the total balance and interest due —and if the machine makes a mistake it shows a red card.

There is in existence of machine weighing about 40 tons which can turn out in a week 400,000 quart bottles or a million pint bottles—to any pattern required.

One man attending 25 machines can turn out 3600 pairs of socks per day.

The Lancashire cotton industry, by working only one full week, can supply the total requirements of Britain for one year.

The Electric Lamp Manufacturing Plant at Corning, New York, can produce 650,000 lamps per machine per day. This represents an increase per man of 10,000 times that of the method previously employed in the industry. (This type of machine can be built by 37 men in six weeks!)

In the Wildwood Colliery near Pittsburgh, two men aided by machines load 1000 tons of coal a day.

According to the Technocracy Energy Survey report from Columbia University in 1932 one man in agriculture can do now in one hour what required 3000 hours to accomplish in 1840.

"Sir Robert Hadfield, in a recent paper (1931) read before the Oil Industries Club, has claimed that economics to the value of £500,000,000 have resulted from the use of two only of the many steels he has invented; while the savings due to Edison's work have been assessed at £4000 million.

"In order to give point to this latter figure, it may be stated that the present annual productivity of the United Kingdom is about £3000 billion; That is, the savings effected by the lifework of *one man* are greater than the present annual output of the second greatest of the industrial nations." (John Hodgson in *The Great God Waste*.)

"Every *week* for the past 20 years my work [Mr. Hodgson is an engineer] has on an average given somebody wealth at a rate of 2500 pounds a *year*. Instead of being able to contemplate with joy the prosperous community that such an increase in industrial efficiency should have brought into being, I am haunted by a wan army of 20,000 unemployed from whom my efficiencies have filched away their life purpose and their means of adequate livelihood." (Ibid.)

"The late Sir George Knibbs estimated after a careful survey that the earth could well support a population four times as great as at present, or about 8000 million." (Dr. R.A. Fisher, of the Statistical Department of the Rothamstead Experimental Station, *Spectator* 7th March, 1931.)

"With the means that science has already placed at our disposal, we might provide for all the wants of each of us in food, shelter and clothing by one hour's work for each of us from school-age to dotage." (Lord Leverhulme: Preface to Professor Spooner's *Wealth From Waste*, 1918)

"That was 15 years ago. In the intervening decade and a half, according to the engineer, J. L.Hodgson, in his paper on *Industrial and Communal Waste* before the Royal Society of Arts on 20th June, 1932, in the course of which he quoted and accepted Lord Leverhulme's statement, 'since that date

our average potential productivity has nearly doubled.' One
half-hour's work per week should thus provide a minimum
standard for all, and one hour's work per week an overwhelming
abundance." (Palme Dutt in *Fascism and Social Revolution*.)

II

Waste and Sabotage (Passive and Active)

2,500,000 acres of English arable land were allowed to
revert to pasturage and went out of cultivation between 1919
and 1930.

60,000 sheep in the San Julian area in the Argentine were
slaughtered and burnt in 1933.

In 1926 the Egyptian Chamber of Deputies passed a law
limiting the cotton acreage for three years to a third of every
plantation.

The Cuban sugar growers recommended their president
to limit 1927's sugar crop two 4,500,000 tons.

In 1933 the USA, Canada, Australia, and the Argentine
agreed to reduce their acreage of wheat by 15%.

The expenditure account recently published of the
Agricultural Adjustment Administration under the Roosevelt
regime affords a pretty picture of modern capitalism (*Economist,*
30th December, 1933):

Expenditures under the A.A.A.:

Allocation	Approximate Sum
Cotton acreage plowed up	$110 million
1934 cotton acreage reduction	$150 million
Emergency pig-sow slaughter	$33 million
Corn-hog production control	$350 million
Wheat acreage reduction	$102 million
Tobacco acreage reduction	$21 million

From Denmark it was reported in November 1933 that cattle were being slaughtered in the government abattoirs at the rate of 5000 a week, for the carcasses to be burnt in the incinerators. The government established a special destruction fund; but so great was the cost of destruction that Parliament had to be approached for further credits for the construction of new slaughterhouses.

The last Labour Government in this country had already carried the Coal Mines Act for the limitation of the output of coal with such success that in the beginning of 1934 a London the firm actually ordered a consignment of coal from abroad, on the grounds, as I stated, that owing to the limitations schemes it was impossible to secure a delivery from British sources with sufficient speed.

The principal copper producers of the world entered into an agreement at Brussels in December 1931, to limit production during 1932 to 26% of the capacity of their mines.

The National Coffee Council of Brazil, from which country comes 2/3 of the world's coffee, decided in December 1931 to destroy 12 million bags of coffee. During 1932-3 1000 248,000,000 pounds were destroyed. Up to the end of 1933 no less them 22 million bags of coffee had been disposed of by burning or dumping in the sea.

The governors of Texas and Oklahoma called on the National Guard to take possession of the oil wells and prevent production.

The United States Department of Agriculture in the summer of 1933 announced bounties of $7-$20 per acre to farmers for the destruction of the cotton crop. This was successful in securing the plowing in or mowing down of 11,000,000 acres out of a total of 40 millions.

"The practical execution of the scheme, however, was not without difficulties, as witness the following item from the American Press on 9th August, 1933:

'Paul A. Porter of the administration, just back from the south, reported today that many farmers had complained they found difficulty in getting their mules to 'act right' while plowing up to cotton. It is not the mule's fault at that, Mr. Porter explained. All these years he has been lambasted if he walked atop the cotton row. Now it is the reverse, and he is being asked to trample down stalks that he was carefully trained to protect.'

"The honors go to the mules rather than to President Roosevelt." (Palme Dutt)

"RAMIE": "Ramie is a fibrous nettle that can be grown with a 22 inch fiber, 1500 pounds to the acre (against cotton's 150 pounds), two or three crops a year possible in the South, harvested like wheat by completely mechanized methods. Spun it makes a cloth seven times as strong as well, several hundred times as strong as cotton. It has luster like silk or linen, and takes dyes beautifully. It is stronger wet than dry. It can be made into light fine paper, too strong to be torn by the human hand. In mass production and the cost of both textile and paper is far below any competing commodity. Here in the real world is the discovery capable of immeasurably raising the standard of living. *But*, the money system is simply not capable of absorbing such a shock. Bankers and moneymen fight Ramie as they fought rayon for 20 years, but ultimately it will break through. Physics is stronger than metaphysics in the long run." (*Attack.*)

"We spend vast skill and ingenuity in digging up, refining, insuring, transporting, assaying and again burying gold. (This 'industry' costs us about £50,000,000 a year.)" (J. Hodgson.)

"In the USA alone about 5 million million linear miles of print –enough to stretch half around the solar system–used, in 'prosperous' times, to appear each year in harmful, degrading and unnecessary advertisements. In industrial societies such as our own, where purchasing power is deliberately limited, 'salesmanship' and advertisement can only divert production from one industry or factory to another. They can never increase its total." (J. Hodgson.)

Outside Sheffield, in one of the largest industrial districts of the world, 50,000,000 ft.³ of coke oven gas—enough to heat all North London—burn to waste every 24 hours. This waste is partly due to the vested interests of the local gas companies, and partly to those who hoped to gain profit by building coke ovens.

White neon tube lighting could now be successfully used for domestic lighting and purposes other than advertising and save a considerable amount of electric current, but it is being withheld on account of vested interests.

"Our 2,500,000 unemployed, if allowed to work at the average rate of productivity of the English worker, could produce for themselves and the community £500,000,000 in additional wealth each year, instead of costing at least 100,000,000 pounds." (J. Hodgson.)

"If we list these various forms of Communal Waste, assess them and add them up, or if we estimate the man-hours efficiently spent that would be necessary to produce the wealth we now enjoy, we have to conclude that at least *9/10 of our activities are at present wasted.*" (J. Hodgson.)

"The Marquess of Donegal in the *Sunday Despatch* tells us Dr. Murray Butler, the President of Columbia University, USA, has pointed out that with the money the last war cost, £800 could have been given to every family in the USA, Canada, Australia, the British Isles, France, Belgium, Russia and Germany!

"On top of this, every town in these countries with a population of over 20,000 could have been supplied with a £1,000,000 library and a £2,000,000 university.

"And then there would be £1000 million leftover!

"If there had been no war, would we have seen anything of all this money? Would every family have got its £800? No, of course not! But why not?

"Houses, furniture and clothes could have been made instead of ammunition. Food could have been eaten instead of destroyed by enemy submarines.

"A new Britain and in new Europe could have been made with the money wasted on the last war." (*Attack.*)

We conclude by closing, again without comment, a letter written to the Editor of the *Financial Chronicle*, USA, 18th August, 1934, which was reprinted in *Attack* under the title *Going the Whole Hog in USA Sabotage*.

"Sir,

"A friend of mine in New England has a neighbor who has received a check for $1000 dollars this year for not raising hogs. So my friend now wants to go into the business himself, he not being very prosperous just now; he says, in fact, that the idea of not raising hogs appeals to him very strongly. Of course, he will need a hired man, and that is where I come in. I write to you as to your opinion of the best kind of farm not to raise hogs on, the best strain of hogs not to raise, and how best to keep an inventory of hogs you are not raising. Also, do you think capital could be raised by insurance of a non-hog-raising gold bond?

The friend who got the thousand dollars got it for not raising 500 hogs. Now we figure we might easily not raise 1500 or 2000 hogs, so you see the possible profits are only limited by the number of hogs we do not raise. The other fellow had been raising hogs for 40 years and never made more than $400 in any one year. Kind of pathetic, isn't it, to think how he wasted his life raising hogs when he could have made so much more by not raising them!

"I will thank you for any advice you may offer.

Yours very truly (signed),

Harold Trurman."

Appendix

Commerce by direct exchange–"clearing"–has come to be an important link in the whole of our modern monetary and credit system. Clearing has been employed at different times, especially during depressions, and has promoted trade independently of money and ordinary credit, which has been restricted on account of the Gold Standard or similar arrangement.

Of late years a number of clearing organizations have been formed in Europe and America and have given rise to a new kind of transaction. An important factor in the case of these undertakings, and one which differentiates them from the various schemes and experiments described in this book, is that they can be private and set up independently of the political authority.

Clearing is normally associated with the politico-commercial agreements reached between different states, as for instance, that between Germany and Italy. Although the principle involved is the same the clearing under discussion here is, however, of rather a different nature and aims at creating a new sort of trading by the side of the old, within countries and between countries reciprocally, by means of direct settlements.

Instead of enumerating the many parts of successful experiments made in this direction in both the Old World and the New, I give here in some detail an account of the single clearing organization formed very recently, namely *The Nordic Clearing Company.* The system in this case has been elaborated by a group of men all prominent in Scandinavian legal and judicial circles. Though its authors have greatly benefited by the accumulated experience of other pioneers it is independent, and distinct from all earlier clearing movements.

The Nordic Clearing Company has its offices in Stockholm, Sweden, and is the central organ for other clearing companies in Sweden, Norway, Denmark, Finland and the Baltic States. Subsidiary organizations are in process of formation also in England, France, Austria, Switzerland, etc. and the object is to work for as extensive an association as possible.

The chairman of the company is the Minister Plenipotentiary Eric Ehrstrom, of Finland. The other directors are: Mr. Sven Runnquist, barrister to the Supreme Court of Appeal, Stockholm; Colonel Carl Eric von Gegerfeldt, Stockholm. Mr. Olaf Dahll, barrister to the Supreme Court of Appeal, Oslo; Captain Alfred Henning and the barrister Ingemar Ullman are vice directors; and Mr. Leif Bamborg, barrister to the Supreme Court of Appeal, Copenhagen, is legal adviser to the company. The company's representative for England is Dr. Thomas Robertson, of Glasgow.

The following are a few arguments written in favor of the movement, in English, by one of its founders;

In his book *Mastering the Crisis* Irving Fisher, LLD, professor of economics at Yale University, speaks of the 'swap idea' and of 'stamp scrip'. On page 151 he says, *'I hope the two will coalesce and solve the "hookup" problem.'*

The Nordic Clearing Regulations are intended to promulgate this 'hookup'. They are contained on a single page, easily comprehended.

Available cash and available credit are one and the same thing, but how many people really understand this?

In some way men have managed to complicate the elementary operation of exchanging their products and their labor. A fatal habit of confusing plus and minus has crept into our economic life and caused havoc. Statistics have become a means to tangles of plotting parasitical thought, serviceable in proving any desired plan or theory.

Interest is paid in a haphazard manner involving great risks and subject to unfair influence.

Through the Clearing Regulations interest will be debited and credited at fixed and definite rates, involving neither risk nor privilege.

Purchasing Power has been at the mercy of uncontrolled whims and speculation and of arbitrary guidance. It is therefore the aim of the Clearing Regulations to restore stable purchasing power to all participators. The banks do clearing of a sort among themselves. Nordic Clearing Regulations attempt to popularize this clearing to include everybody.

At the present time money credits (ordinary credits) are arbitrarily liquidated, causing constant periods of crisis and the bankruptcy of some 0-odd percent of all business every 16 years.

Credits issued according to the Nordic Clearing Regulations also have to be liquidated, but instead of exposing the users of the credit to bankruptcy and other conditions unworthy of our civilization, an orderly and gradual liquidation is provided for through an insurance charge made against all transfers. Orderly liquidation must result and the term debt assumes an entirely different significance. Debts will no longer be an oppressive burden but rather a self-consuming fuel necessary to the interchange of human sustenance. The old kind of debt has become an unbearable burden because of its imposed self-increasing quality, under the guise of an uncontrolled factor known under the name of 'interest'.

So far the problem of the necessary credit to carry on, and of circulating this credit, has been left to the more or less credit-rationed banks and to advertising agencies. Where these leave off is the intention that the clearing practice should supplement and continue.

The following is drawn from a pamphlet by various men actively engaged in Nordic Clearing, recently published in Sweden and Norway.

History affords the spectacle of a number of different

periods when economic activities seriously decreased and the whole economic mechanism retrogressed. Sometimes this was attributed to a total or partial failure of crops or to underproduction of other goods. At other times these crises occurred without any initial decrease in production. Vast stocks of commodities lay unsold while a good proportion of the labor and population was unemployed, in spite of the fact that people needed the goods available and were ready to offer their services in exchange for them.

This last kind of depression may be called a *trade or distributive crisis*. We have recently experienced a crisis of this description, more striking and more characteristic than preceding crises of a like nature, since we now have a greater surplus of goods and above all greater productive power than formerly.

It is not our object to discuss the causes of trade crises, nor to deal generally with the different measures with which they might be met, but to point out that private institutions, sprung from ordinary commercial life, have, during earlier crises been of very great use.

The first clearing banks, from which our present bank and credit system has developed greatly assisted commerce, in that they permitted settlements on the security of deposits.

A number of institutions have, however, gone still further: they have allowed settlements purely on the security of values in the form of goods and services available, without the safeguard of actual deposits. A typical example is the Bonnard Bank. Opened in the year 1849 after the depression in France with headquarters in Marseilles and branch offices in Paris and Lyons, this firm served as a kind of Exchange or Center of barter, where producers, wholesalers, merchants and wage earners of every description could meet for the direct exchange of goods and services. The bank issued 'credit notes', by means of which the interested parties were able to exchange their goods and services on a scale which far surpassed what could be done at that time through ordinary commercial channels.

This bank enjoyed such great confidence that, on the average, it refused daily four times as much business as it was able to undertake. During the course of its first three years of trading the Paris office of the firm undertook commissions worth 127 million francs (an equivalent of 635 million francs today) practically without the use of currency and *without incurring a single loss*. A catalog from 1857 of the purveyors and enrolled occupies 64 pages.

It seems to be generally admitted that this bank really did promote new trade and did not merely deprive its orthodox competitors of a certain proportion of their business. Financial periodicals and publications referred to this special bank with great sympathy and goodwill. The firm is still extant and is managed by the founder's grandson. Apart from its bartering activities the bank now deals with ordinary business.

The present trade crisis should more than any preceding it favor the rise of similar enterprises. We now have richer resources, greater productive capacity and more experience at our command than ever before. Moreover we have a better grasp of distributive problems than formerly. Numberless projects and practical experiments afford ample information for the setting up of practicable clearing organizations. In America these barter centers or exchange companies have enjoyed a great boom of recent years. They have given permanent employment to tens of thousands of people and millions have benefited by their activities.

A European enterprise of this kind is *The Nordic Clearing Company*, the object of which is to promote the exchange of goods and services within countries and between different countries reciprocally, and also to organize reciprocal credits to the help of cooperating clearing companies in different countries.

Local companies are in process of formation in Norway, Sweden, and Denmark, to be followed by similar organizations in Finland, Iceland and the Baltic States. Together these countries will form a ring. Plans are now also being laid for establishing clearing companies in England, France, Belgium,

Austria, Hungary, Switzerland and other countries, which will join the association, the object being by this means to develop the system into an extensive international commercial organization.

The System to be adopted is based on the experience of earlier experimenters and, moreover, offers many valuable suggestions deriving from the latest observations.

THE FORMATION OF LOCAL COMPANIES

The procedure when starting a local department of the Nordic Clearing Company is as follows:

Relations are entered into with producers, merchants and wage earners. As soon as a sufficiently representative number of members is enrolled operations may immediately commence.

Each member contributes to certain sum of money to cover running expenses and as a basis of credit. This money, however, is not idle capital for the party may at once have a clearing account opened for the sum in question, i.e. he can for this sum immediately obtain goods and services from other members or from outsiders wishing to trade with the company. Since it may be assumed that each member would want to make an immediate use of his credit the sum contributed is at once turned over and becomes the instrument of continually fresh transactions. The seller delivering goods against an order on the buyer's clearing credit is himself credited with the sum in question, of which he can again make an immediate use.

Experience has shown that when a sum has been introduced into the clearing system it quickly and surely mediates new transactions.

Provided there is a sufficiently large roll of original members the specified entrance fee and credit cover may be fixed as low as 50 Crowns (about 50 shillings) per member. The total amount thus collected should be sufficient to set the undertaking on its feet. Additional cleaning creditors is obtained in the following ways:

1. By depositing fresh cash, for which a premium of 5% is allowed. This premium increases the purchasing power of the members and is justifiable and economically beneficial in a time of constantly expanding productive capacity; moreover it is of such modest proportions that clearing companies have always shown themselves able to afford it with ease by employing a liquidation or amortization system to be described later.

On the other hand no interest in the ordinary sense is paid by the company against cash payments since they are immediately turned into goods or services, the idea being not to deposit cash before it is actually needed for purchase.

Furthermore a bonus is given or discount allowed on each purchase and this stresses even more the company's character of a purely distributive organization. The company is not intended as repository of money in competition with banks.

2. The Company shall also grant members credit without cash, but to begin with against ordinarily accepted securities.

LIQUIDATION OF CREDITS. BUYERS' BONUS

The credit which is transferred from one member to another in the form of goods delivered or services rendered is as a rule repaid with goods and services at no interest and within a period convenient to both parties. Debtors who deposit cash are assured of a fresh credit, i.e. an immediate right to goods or services, for the whole value of the deposit.

Furthermore credit amortises itself in the course of business. This comes about in the following way: for every transaction the seller is debited with the discount of 1/2% for amounts of £2000 or over, rising to 5% on amounts under 50 Crowns. A clearing transaction is for the seller practically speaking equivalent to a cash sale at a minimum risk, and, moreover, he is provided, as it were, with free marketing service, since it is the company which puts purchasers in touch with suppliers. Thus the discount is merely a fair fee and a small one. It should be debited to the seller since a member is best able to bear this expense at the moment he makes a sale. As the members are alternately buyers and sellers all share in bearing this cost.

The amount deducted in discounts is allocated in the company's books in the following way: one third goes back to the buyer and is credited to his account, i.e. amortizes his credit. Thus credit is gradually and automatically liquidated in the course of business. At the rate of turnover, which experience has shown may be reckoned with, amortization proceeds with remarkable rapidity (see later). Another third of all discounts goes to covering the company's administration costs, to liquidating its possible debts, or to forming a reserve. The remaining one third is, during the first two years' activities, credited as commission to those responsible for enrolling new members, but after such period this practice is dispensed with and the whole two-thirds of the sellers' discounts go to the company. After some time income from this source will considerably exceed the company's needs of the surplus obtained will be distributed to each member in proportion to his contribution to the total turnover. This supplements the amortization of credit and can eventually form the basis of new and extended credit for the members.

CASH PAYMENTS

Cash which lies at the disposal of the company and is not needed for purposes of administration, may also be loaned out to members in need of ready money, as for instance, those needing materials which cannot be obtained by direct exchange within the organization. In the case of these cash loans there is in the first place deducted from the borrower's account that 5% bonus credited to him against his original deposit and in the second place 5% is charged on the loan as security to cover risks of nonpayment. Ordinary interest is not demanded.

ORDINARY PROCEDURE

For daily transactions an order or check system is as a rule adopted. The company issues books of regulation printed forms, in order that the work of accounting shall be as homogenous and a simple as possible. A member may draw orders up to an amount corresponding to the credit which he holds. The buyer fills in a form stating the amount of his purchase, together with his name and that of the supplier. When the buyer has signed the order it is handed to the seller who has his account credited with the value of the goods or services furnished, after the specified sales discount has been deducted. The buyer's account is debited with the sum in question and credited with his share of the discount. At the same time the company's account is credited with its share and the balance if need be credited as commission to those members responsible for recruiting new members.

The company shall keep the catalog of all purveyors who have subscribes to the organization and a copy shall be furnished to any member on demand.

PRICE VARIATIONS

Credits are automatically regulated in accordance with any change in the price index. In this way members are always assured of the same real purchasing power, irrespective of fluctuations in the value of money.

VELOCITY OF CIRCULATION–INCREASED TURNOVER

Experience has shown that clearing much encourages a quick turnover. In the case of the clearing movement in Germany and France circulation rate has been 100 per annum. A curious instance in this connection is that of an experiment conducted a public meeting held in Bâle. 10 Francs were distributed to each of the three unemployed men (30 Francs in all) on the understanding that they should immediately dispose of the money in exchange for goods offered by sellers present who had declared their willingness to allow cash discounts in view of the cash payment. The sellers in their turn immediately spent the same sum on goods offered by other sellers and so on. Delivery was to take place later but the transactions were completed on the spot. The giver of the original 30 Francs was to receive the total of the cash discounts allowed. The suppliers present were subsequently asked how large a cash discount each had given, and it transpired that they had allowed from 2-20% or 5% on the average. *In the course of 40 minutes these 30 Francs turned over goods worth about 600 francs and the original donor was refunded 26.7 Francs in the form of cash discounts.* His gift of 30 Francs, had, after becoming a credit, that's yielded almost 100% in less than one hour. The credit had 'amortized itself' during this time, and the 30 francs had circulated 20 times within 40 minutes.

Such an increased velocity of circulation naturally brings with it an increased total turnover. Herein lies the main task of the clearing system, viz. an expansion of the total volume of trade done within the community, as well as the exploitation of energy and productivity available to meet existing unsatisfied needs. It is the object of the company not to assume the functions of other institutions and compete with them but purely to bring about new trade by means largely of bartering.

That there are no opportunities for, and a need of, such new trade should be sufficiently well-known. To quote a small instance it might be mentioned that during the depression in the USA credits amounting to $20 milliard have been withdrawn since 1929, which is equivalent to say that trade has decreased by a corresponding amount, without the occurrence of any relative decrease in productive power, supplies are from materials or of human needs—in fact, rather the contrary.

Clearing can, owing to its peculiar nature, be as good as independent variations in monetary circuit-velocity and of ordinary restrictions of credit.

States, municipalities, parishes and other corporate bodies can in the capacity of producers and consumers join a clearing company, thus making it possible for payments of taxes, water and electricity rates, etc. to go through a clearing organization.

In Denmark an investigation has already been carried out of what clearing would mean to the inhabitants of the town of Aarhus and to the affairs of the municipality, if the latter (1) partially adopted a clearing policy, or (2) in the course of a 20 year liquidation period went in exclusively for clearing. This investigation showed that the municipality would gradually become free of debts, that the burden of taxes would be reduced and unemployment diminish.

The following, reprinted by kind permission of the A/B Nordisk Clearing, are the Regulations issued for the use of English companies in the Nordic Clearing System:

A/B NORDISK CLEARING

CLEARING REGULATIONS

1. A clearing-credit account can be opened by application to any clearing office in the A/B Nordisk Clearing organization.

An account is opened against payment of an amount fixed by the local clearing office to serve, wholly or partly, as the desired initial credit basis.

2. Further credit is granted as follows:

(a) Against presentation of orders of transfer from the holder of an account with the clearing office under A/B Nordisk Clearing (see 4.);

(b) against approved security;

(c) against transfer of acceptance or other claims on third parties. When such claims are paid in cash a 5% bonus is credited to the holder of the account;

(d) against payment in cash. Credit is then obtained for the amount deposited, plus a bonus of 5%.

Whoever obtains clearing credit under "(b)" must, until otherwise decided by A/B Nordisk Clearing, within a time limit fixed in each particular case by the respective clearing office, deposit a corresponding cash sum.

The amount of such cash, plus a 5% bonus, is, in accordance with the request of the borrower, applied either to the expansion of the borrower's credit or to liquidation of the borrowers debt (see 8.).

3. Credit amounts can be transferred between accounts in offices under A/B Nordisk Clearing, but are not payable in cash. Transfers are generally made through clearing-transfer orders presented for credit to the account (see 2.a.) of the holder of the order and for the debit to the accounts of the drawer of the order. The name of the receiver of the

transfer order must be filled in at the time of the signing of the transfer order.

Transfer orders are non-endorsable and must be presented direct to the clearing office within 10 days. The transfer orders can be certified for credit by the clearing office. At the same time the amount is blocked on the account of the giver of the order.

4.   On every amount transferred the account of the receiver of the order is debited with a turnover charge (sales discount), calculated as follows:

1/2% on amounts above 1000 Sw. Kr., minimum 1000 ore.

1% on amounts from 1000 to 250 Sw. Kr., minimum 750 ore.

3% on amounts from 250 to 50 Sw. Kr., minimum 250 ore.

5% on amounts under 50 Sw. Kr., minimum 15 ore.

5. The distribution of the turnover charge (sales discount) is as follows:

(a) one third is immediately credited to an amortization and savings column in the account of the drawer of the clearing-transfer order. Transfer from this column to the clearing credit column of the drawer's account can take place when he has settled his obligation to the clearing office or when the clearing office consents to such transfer.

(B) two thirds is credited to the administration account of the clearing office.

After deduction for the administrative expenses, reserve fund, depreciation fund, general fund and dividends to stockholders the surplus is at the end of the fiscal year credited to the amortization and savings accounts of the account holders in proportion to the total turnover charge debited and credited to each account during the preceding year.

6.   The liquid assets of the Clearing Office, in as far as they are not required for the use of the office itself, are at the disposal of the account owners as loans against acceptable security.

Loans are granted against acceptable security and are remitted according to separate agreements in each particular case.

When the amount of the loan is paid out 10% is deducted. Half of this deduction (5%) serves as a guarantee for the return of the cash and is returned to the clearing account of the borrower when the money is returned. The other half of the 10% is then credited to the borrower as a bonus according to 2.d.

7. Clearing credit accounts, amortization and savings accounts (credit-regulating accounts), as well as the loan accounts (see 6.) are stabilized and regulated in the amortization and savings accounts according to a price index figure approved by A/B Nordisk Clearing, whenever this index shows a variation. This regulation starts when the said price index shows a variation of at least 20% from the 1st September, 1935.

8. Clearing credits are generally amortized through transfers from the amortization and savings account (see 5.) If an account owner wishes to withdraw deposited security or fails to meet contracted engagements to the Clearing Office or is otherwise guilty of misconduct, payment of his indebtedness can be exacted in cash (see 7.) at the demand of the Clearing Office.

9. A/B Nordisk Clearing is exclusively authorized to use the Nordisk Clearing Credit System.

Changes in, or in addition to, these regulations can be made only by A/B Nordisk Clearing, whose decisions on the interpretation of any of the above regulations are final.

BIBLIOGRAPHY

THE "FREE" ECONOMISTS

Gesell, Silvio: *Die Natürliche Wirtschaftsirdnung durch Friesland und Freigold.*

Schwartz, Fritz: *Vorwärts zur festen Kauftkrat des Geldes und zur zinsbefreiten Wirtschaft*

AN ENERGY THEORY OF WEALTH

Soddy, Frederick: *Wealth, Virtual Wealth and Debt*

TECHNOCRACY

Arkwright: *What is Technocracy?*

Scott, Howard: *Introduction to Technocracy*

SOCIAL CREDIT

Douglas, Clifford Hugh: *The Douglas Manual; Economic Democracy; Control and Distribution of Production; Credit-Power and Democracy; The Monopoly of Credit; Social Credit; Warning Democracy*

Hattersley, C. Marshall: *This Age of Plenty*

Holter, E.S.: *A.B.C. of Social Credit*

Millar og Murstad: *Økonomisk Frigjorelse (Douglasplanen)*

Various Writers: Pamphlets on the New Economics

STABILIZED MONEY

Eisler, Robert: *Stable Money*

Fisher, Irving: *The Money Illusion; Booms and Depressions* (1933); *Stabilized Money* (1935)

Sweden's Experiment: *Index of Svenska Handelsbaken* n. 81 (Sept. 1932) Bertil Ohlin; *Skandinaviske Kredittaktiebolaget, Quarterly Report,* July 1933 (Cassel); *Economic Forum,* Juni-Juli 1934 (Eric Lindahl)

Vregille, Gonzague de: *Les Banques fonctionnant sans métal précieux permettent-elles de parler d'un mythe d'or?*

THE READER IS ALSO REFERRED TO THE FOLLOWING:

Colbjörnsen og Sömme: *En norsk Trearsplan*

Damaschke: *What everybody wants to know about money*

Dufayel, Henri: *Banque*

Ebengreuth: *Allgemeine Münzkunde und Geldeschiehte des Mittelalters*

Ely, Richard: *Nationalökonomien i Grundgrekk (dansk utg)*

Frisch, Ragnar: *Sparing og cirkulasnonsregulering*

Francé: *Der Weg der Kultur*

Freytag: *Bildern aus der Deutschen Vergangenheit*

Haldane, J.B.S.: *Possible Worlds*

Hiskett, W.R.: *Social Credit or Socialism*

Keilhau: *Overgang til ny pengeenhet*

Keynes: *A Treatise on Money*

Marshall, Alfred: *Principles of Economics*

Nielsen, Axel: *Bankpolitikk II*

Roosevelt: *Looking Forward*

Shaw, D.W.: *Currency, Credit and the Exchanges during the Great War*

Sinding: *Samfundsökonomi*

Somme, L.J.: *Det gamle negative pengesystems undergang etc.*

Valeur: *Et Frigort samfund*

Winter-Hjelm, Thorof: *Kapitalrente og Agerrente*

Divers böker fra, Det Frie samfunds forlag

Acknowledgements

This edition of *Distribute or Destroy: A Survey of the World's Glut of Goods with a Description of Various Proposals and Practical Experiments for its Distribution* has been published as it was originally written by Brynjolf Björset, translated to English by I.R. and E.S. de Mare.

We are grateful to Diane Feught for her insightful cover design and to Joe Clare, patron of the arts and humanity, for his support for the production of this edition.

Thanks are also due to Jim Dempsey for verifying some of the details in this volume and for his continued interest in Shamcher's work in energy and economics.

Distribute or Destroy is a publication of the Shamcher Archives, dedicated to preserving and publishing the works of Shamcher Bryn Beorse. It was first published in English in 1936 by Stanley Nott Ltd. London.

The Norwegian original publication, *Efter Oss Kommer Overfloden*, was published by Aschehoug, Oslo, Norway, in 1934.

Find background to the book, reference links, further details and other books by Shamcher Bryn Beorse at:

www.distribute-or-destroy.shamcher.com

ABOUT THE AUTHOR

Born in Norway in 1896, Brynjolf Björset later emigrated to the US, shortening his name to Bryn Beorse(1896-1980). He authored many non-fiction books, novels and articles, covering topics of energy, economics, full employment, and global awareness as well as yoga and Sufism.

He worked and travelled in over 65 countries in his lifetime. Fluent in several languages, his comprehensive worldview included the inner meditative life as well as the accomplishment of life in the world. Sent on a UN economic mission to Tunisia in the 1960's, helping to rebuild the Norwegian economy after WWII, Beorse also spent time in exploration, travelling to the Kumbha Mela in India, living in the dunes of Oceano, and going to China at the time of the revolution. A spy in WWII, he was part of the plot to kidnap Hitler. An advocate of the giro-credit economic system, he spoke out against the stagnation of hierarchical organization.

An accomplished yogi and Sufi, (known as Shamcher) he was instrumental in developing Sufi centres throughout the world, in the tradition of Inayat Khan. He dedicated the last years of his life to OTEC, Ocean Thermal Energy Conversion, a source of benign solar power from the sea. He passed away in Berkeley, California in 1980.

More info at: www.shamcher.org

www.ingramcontent.com/pod-product-compliance
Lightning Source LLC
Chambersburg PA
CBHW071554200326
41519CB00021BB/6743